Books writt

Trust Goc

What Wil

Never, Never Give Up

How to Study the Bible

Quiet Confidence in the Lord

One Hundred Years from Today

Nuggets of Faith

God's Will for Your Life

Books co-authored by Jack and Judy Hartman

A Close and Intimate Relationship with God

God's Joy Regardless of Circumstances

Victory Over Adversity

What Does God Say?

Receive Healing from the Lord

Unshakable Faith in Almighty God

Exchange Your Worries for God's Perfect Peace

God's Wisdom Is Available to You

Increased Energy and Vitality

Scripture Meditation Cards co-authored by Jack and Judy Hartman

Receive Healing from the Lord

Freedom from Worry and Fear

Enjoy God's Wonderful Peace

God Is Always with You

Continually Increasing Faith in God

Receive God's Blessings in Adversity

Financial Instructions from God

Find God's Will for Your Life

A Closer Relationship with the Lord

Our Father's Wonderful Love

We pray this book will bless you abundantly. Yours in Christ Jack + Judy

COMMENTS FROM READERS OF OUR PUBLICATIONS

The following are just a few of the comments contained in more than seven hundred letters we have received pertaining to our publications. For additional comments, see our website: lamplight.net.

Trust God for Your Finances

- "We find your material to be so readable and upbuilding. Your writing communicates a clear and fatherly concern for the edification of the believer. *Trust God for Your Finances* is a tremendous book. Your book by far is the most thorough and systematic work I have read to date. The church here in Greece has a great need for this book." (Greece) (This book was translated into Greek.)
- "I have translated *Trust God for Your Finances* into Thai. My pastor asked for 700 copies to distribute at the special yearly conference for pastors. More than 1,000 people attended the conference. Seven hundred copies were distributed to only the pastors, elders and deacons who really wanted the book. After the conference, we had so many calls that another 2,000 copies were printed. Thank you, Mr. Hartman, for this book which is helping so many Thai Christians." (Thailand)
- "Today we had a ministry partner join us for lunch. He said that the book, *Trust God for Your Finances*, that we had translated into Hebrew was the most powerful book he had ever read on the subject. I shared with him the wonderful story of how you shared the book with us and how many Israelis have been enlightened in that area as a result of reading the book. You both are a blessing and a treasure in God's kingdom." (Israel)

What Will Heaven Be Like?

- "On the very first page of your book on heaven I was spellbound. The material read so quickly and coherently that it was like having a conversation with a Christian friend. I could really feel the excitement as we talked about the throne of God and its radiance. Those who are curious about heaven will be so delighted and joyful when they read this book. I think the questions at the end of the book are a great idea. This book is a ready-made classroom treasure. I was deeply moved by the gentle loving approach and the manner this material was presented to me, the reader. I can hardly wait to read your other books. You have gained a new fan and admirer of your special way of presenting the kingdom of heaven and God's love for us." (Mississippi)

- "I came to China from Cambodia where I was a captain in the army. I was a Buddhist. Four weeks before I came to China, I had a dream where Jesus appeared to me. When I woke up the following morning, I looked for Christians to explain more about Jesus Christ to me. After I came to China, I met a Christian man who gave me the book *What Will Heaven Be Like?*. This book answered many questions for me. My English is not very good, but this book is written in very simple English. I have found new life through this book. Please pray for me so that I can share Jesus with my parents and my Buddhist friends when I go back to Cambodia." (China)

- "I am the Youth Director of our church and I'm leading a group of high school students in a Bible study of your book on heaven. We all respect your opinions and have found your book to be an excellent springboard for discussion. It is thought-provoking and informative. This book has much substance and is well organized." (California)

Never, Never Give Up
- "When I received your book *Never, Never Give Up*, all was well in my life. I was supposed to be married when I graduated from the higher institution of learning, but this marriage never materialized. The lady I loved so much suffered from migraine headaches and eye pain. She suffered in great pain for almost a year and then she died. In all of this journey of suffering I read your book three times. The contents are so meaningful to me and built a good strong character in me. Though my fiancé died and went to be with the Lord, God saw me through that problem. *Never, Never Give Up* was a timely book. It is written simply and is easy to understand. I pray that the Lord will continue to use your ministry to help people who are going through a tough time." (Zambia)

- "Thanks for being there when you are so much needed by all of us. After seven major operations I am beginning to walk again and help others which is the full purpose of my existence which Jesus Christ has set before me. Your book, *Never, Never Give Up*, stayed by my pillow along with my Bible while I was recuperating from these operations. When I re-read it, I was charged with peace and energy again. The pain diminishes and I can speak of God's infinite love and mercy to others who are facing similar trials. Thank you for writing this God-inspired book." (Florida)
- "Suicide has shown its face in my mind. I found myself falling deeper and deeper into the pit of hell. My life seemed so grim. I could not see where I could make a difference and was planning to believe that if I chose to leave this life it would not matter. When I received *Never, Never Give Up* I read the first three chapters that evening. When I arrived at page ninety, your verse changed my life. I want you to know that I have been delivered from this season of trial. I rededicated my life to the Lord and feel wonderful. Thank you so much for your work. Through our Lord you have saved my life. Thank you for my life back." (Texas)

God's Joy Regardless of Circumstances

- "*God's Joy Regardless of Circumstances* came to me right on time. Being in prison for twenty years for a crime I didn't commit and then having to deal with severe family problems is not a morsel that is easy to swallow. My oldest daughter was pregnant and we were looking forward to having my first grandson born. We were very pained to learn that my daughter had to lose her baby. In the midst of dealing with this problem, you sent me a free copy of *God's Joy Regardless of Circumstances*. When I avidly started to read this book, my daughter underwent surgery, lost her baby and faced uncertainty and despair. *God's Joy Regardless of Circumstances* pulled us through. Thank you also for sending a free copy of this book to my daughter. May God continue blessing Lamplight Ministries." (Florida)
- "Many thanks for sending me *God's Joy Regardless of Circumstances*. This book has been a real stream in the desert that I have been able to drink from. I have been blessed tremendously by this book. My life has not been the same since I started reading it. I have used this book to help many people on my radio

programme every Sunday. Many people have given their lives to Christ because of these messages." (Zambia)

- "I read *God's Joy Regardless of Circumstances* at a time when the devil was doing everything he could to steal my joy. I was desperate. I learned that the circumstances in my life have no bearing on God's promises. I have learned that I can live in God's joy no matter what my circumstances dictate. This book showed me step-by-step the way back to the joy that I had lost. You have caused Scripture that I have known since I was a child to come alive with new meaning. This book is wonderful. Thank you so much for the great encouragement you have given to me." (Florida)

Quiet Confidence in the Lord

- "As soon as I was diagnosed with prostate cancer I began to meditate on the Scripture and your explanation of the Scripture in *Quiet Confidence in the Lord*. I carried this book with me everywhere for several weeks. The specialist at the Lahey Clinic in Boston told me I was the calmest person with this diagnosis that he had ever seen. During the pre-op and the surgery a number of people commented on how calm I was. I experienced a lot of discomfort during the difficult first week at home after the surgery. I focused constantly on the Scripture in this wonderful book. I was remarkably calm. Thank you for writing this book that has helped me so much." (Massachusetts)

- "After I graduated from Bible school, I went outside of my country for mission work with my wife. After we were there for nine months, my wife died suddenly. My sorrow was great. I read your book titled *Quiet Confidence in the Lord*. This book spoke to my heart. All twenty-three chapters were written for me. God changed me through this book and comforted me and took away my sorrow. Through the blood of Jesus I entered into God's rest. I can give a great recommendation for this book to anyone who is filled with sorrow and grief. I pray that many people will read this book and develop quiet confidence in the Lord as I did. Thank you so much for sending this book to me. May God bless you and your ministry." (Ethiopia)

- "*Quiet Confidence in the Lord* is with me at work each day. I read and underlined passages that lift my heart and help me to understand something I've known all along and that is that I am not alone and that God cares very much that I'm in the midst of great adversity. I asked God to send me a comforter, someone who would put their arms around me and say, 'I understand and I care.' The answer to that prayer is in you and Judy. Thanks to *Quiet Confidence of the Lord* I am, for the first time in my life, learning to focus on God and not my problems. Thank you both for your ministry. Your books are a tremendous blessing to hurting people all over the world." (Washington, DC)

What Does God Say?

- "Our Sunday School class meets for two hours each Sunday before the regular church service. We have discussed six or seven of your previous books in past classes. *What Does God Say?* is the best one yet. The response from the people in our class has been phenomenal. We begin each class by asking people to state their biggest problems. Once the problems of the members of the class are defined, we choose which of the 94 topics to discuss. The people in our class are telling other people about this book and new people are joining our class." (Iowa)

- "I have never seen a book like *What Does God Say?*. This is more than a book – it is a complete manual. I am very blessed by the way you have simplified this book. I preach from this book on Sundays, Tuesdays, Fridays and Saturdays. It is always with me so I can preach or teach to any group without notice. I thank God for you and I thank Him for your ministry which has helped many people here." (Zambia)

- "*What Does God Say?* has truly blessed the members of our church. Each topic is presented in clear and simple text supported by the Word of God. This book is filled with solutions to life's problems. I appreciate your commitment and dedication to God in making His Word available to so many people who truly need to hear the pure Gospel. This book is very much needed. I do not have words to express my sincere gratitude. You have been a blessing to us. Our members will profit and grow from this book. I am praying for you both. God bless you." (Texas)

Exchange Your Worries for God's Perfect Peace

- "*Exchange Your Worries for God's Perfect Peace* is a masterpiece. I am reading this book to the people here in the Philippines.

I saw tears flowing down their faces as I read them parts of this book. I must get this book translated into their language. I am reading this book for the second time. After thirty years in the ministry I have finally learned how to turn my worries over to God. I have learned more from this book in the last few months than I have ever learned in my life. I will not allow my copy of this book to leave my presence. I thank God for you." (Philippines)

- "I just want to tell you how much I appreciate you and your excellent book, *Exchange Your Worries for God's Perfect Peace*. I have read all of your books several times each. I continually go back to refer to the notes I have made in your books. I have done this for close to fifteen years and pages are falling out of your books. I read the Bible daily. Your books are a close second to the Bible. I have never found another Christian author who teaches me more about God's Word and speaks directly to my heart as your writings do. Thank you for helping me appreciate and respect the Word of God." (Wisconsin)
- "I was in despair struggling with my life and ministry. *Exchange Your Worries for God's Perfect Peace* has strengthened me and encouraged my heart. My country is often threatened by disasters. Your book and the Scripture in it has helped me to focus on God, no matter what circumstances I have experienced and will face in the future. The language in the book is very clear and easy to understand for someone like me who uses English as a second language. I have been blessed by reading this book. My faith in Jesus has increased. Thank you for sending this book to me. I thank God that I know you. You are a blessing." (Indonesia)

God's Wisdom Is Available to You
- "I did not sleep last night after reading your book *God's Wisdom is Available to You*. Thank you for your wonderful work. Because of persecution against my ministry, I spent a considerable amount of time in the hospital because of depression. I am now well and healthy in Jesus' name. Thank you for your help. I will be teaching members of my church from key text in your book. Please be my mentor, teacher and counselor." (Ghana)
- I thank God each and every day for Jack and Judy Hartman. When I started reading your book on wisdom, everything was going wrong in my life. This book revived my spirit and my faith in God.

It has changed my life. The Bible used to be like Greek to me. Now I can read it and understand it. I can't put this book down because I know I need to absorb it. I'm going through it for a second time. This book is one of the best things that has ever happened to me. I thank you both and I thank God." (Florida)

- "You did a fantastic job on this book. It is an encyclopedia on God's wisdom. The writing style is just great. Many books don't bring the reader through the subject the way this book does. I'm very impressed with that. You have made it a real joy for me to study and re-digest Scripture. This book has been very good for me." (North Carolina)

How to Study the Bible

- "Your book, *How to Study the Bible*, is a gem. Since I became a Christian 41 years ago, I have studied the Bible using a variety of methods. Your method is simple and straightforward. It involves hard work, but the rewards are real. I have read several of your books and this book is the one I would highly recommend to any Christian because this book is the foundation. God bless you, brother." (England)

- "My wife and I are utilizing the Bible study method that you explained in *How to Study the Bible*. We are really growing spiritually as a result. Our old methods of study were not nearly as fruitful. Thank you for writing about your method." (Idaho)

- "I have read almost all of your books and they are outstanding. The one that blessed me the most was *How to Study the Bible*. The study part was excellent, but the meditation chapters were very, very beneficial. I am indebted to you for sharing these. I purchased 30 copies to give to friends. Every earnest student of God's Word needs a copy." (Tennessee)

Unshakable Faith in Almighty God

- "*Unshakable Faith in Almighty God* has amazed me. The language is so simple and very clear to understand. This book is powerful and life-changing. I will always hang on to this book. Brother Hartman, God's favour and wisdom are so great on your life. I believe this book is written on very heavy anointing from God. Your reward in heaven will be so great. All those who have sown seeds in your ministry should rejoice. When I wake up, I read this book. Before going to bed, I read it. I will continue to go through it again and again. Your ministry is a big blessing to me. You are always in our prayers." (Zambia)

- "As a minister, missionary and Bible school executive for some sixty years, I would like to comment on your wonderful book, *Unshakable Faith in Almighty God*. You are right on. You are raising a voice that needs to be heard by every Christian in the day in which we live. It is a voice of warning and is also a voice that carries with it a solution for the drama facing the church today. The average Christian is not prepared in the one thing needed to survive the future, an unfailing faith based on saturation in the Word of God." (Florida)

- "If there is one thing that people need above all else it is *Unshakable Faith in Almighty God*. Next to my Bible, I put this book among the best. Every reader should place this book next to his or her Bible. Hundreds of Scripture references that support the challenging truths in this book will equip readers for the future. We want to help get your writings into the hands of people in the island nations. Thank you for being so obedient to the Lord. Thank you for the time and the energy that you have invested in the lives of so many." (Australia)

Victory Over Adversity

- "Your book, *Victory over Adversity*, is great. This book is very complete and easy to understand. I liked it so much that I already have read it two times and I will continue to refer to it often. This book has it all. You have done the work for us. Any person facing adversity of any sort can find specific answers from the Bible in your book. I now know that nothing can come against me that God has not already provided for. Thank you so much for your encouragement." (Iowa)

- "I am 84 years old. I am believing God for healing of macular degeneration. I can only read with one eye, but I was so excited about *Victory over Adversity* that I read the entire book with one eye. This book is awesome. I hated to see it come to an end. All of your books have been a great help to me. God bless you." (New Hampshire)

- "Recently a severe problem caused my heart to sink. Fear came into my life. I often woke up in the middle of the night overwhelmed with fear. *Victory over Adversity* was life-saving. This book is another master work. I read Chapter 4 again and again. Chapter 5 helped me to turn this problem over to God Who knows exactly what to do with problems that seem to be impossible to solve. Thank you for lifting my spirits and helping me to see God instead of adversity." (Philippines)

Receive Healing from the Lord

- "Your great book, *Receive Healing from the Lord*, has amazed me. This book has been my daily bread. I have followed all of God's instructions in your book. My children and my wife were healed from severe illness. I was sick myself just before an important crusade. I meditated on the Scripture in your book for the entire night. I was totally healed. The following day God did wonders as He healed many people. Since then, people have been coming to receive their healing at our home and church almost every day. Many healings are taking place at our services. This book is wonderful. I am abundantly blessed by it." (Zambia)

- "All of the books that you sent us have been given away. Notable was the testimony of a pastor who was healed as a result of reading *Receive Healing from the Lord*. This brother was in failing health for the last three years. When I met him this year he was really weak. I perceived that numerous worries were choking his faith so I gave him four of your books. The situation of this pastor was quite bad last month. He had mistakenly consumed wrong medication which led to partial blindness and joint pain. He could not move. He called to tell me about his sudden healing. I could not believe it. I was quite apprehensive. I asked him to meet me at the bus station. To my amazement he came riding a bicycle. He narrated to me the story of how he was healed after reading *Receive Healing from the Lord*. This man of God is now strong. It is the Lord. God richly bless you." (Zambia)

- "I am so blessed by your comprehensive book on divine healing. This book is a monumental masterpiece. The Holy Ghost has written this book. Glory be to God that you have obeyed Him. You have presented dynamic scriptural instructions for Christians who are sick that will enable them to progressively increase their faith for divine healing. You obviously have put a lot of labor into this book. Many people will be blessed by it." (Florida)

COMMENTS ON OUR SCRIPTURE MEDITATION CARDS

- "My back was hurting so badly that I couldn't get comfortable. I was miserable whether I sat or stood or laid down. I didn't know what to do. Suddenly I thought of the Scripture cards on healing that my husband had purchased. I decided to meditate on the Scripture in these cards. I was only on the second card when, all of a sudden, I felt heat go from my neck down through my body. The Lord had healed me. I never knew it could happen so fast. The pain has not come back." (Idaho)

- "My wife and I use your Scripture cards every day when we pray. I read the card for that day in English and then my wife repeats it in Norwegian. We then pray based upon the Scripture reference on that day's card. These cards have been very beneficial to us. We would like to see the Scripture cards published in the Norwegian language." (Norway)

- "Your Scripture cards have been very helpful to my wife and myself. We have taped them to the walls in our home and we meditate on them constantly. I also take four or five cards with me every day when I go to work. I meditate on them while I drive. The Scripture on these cards is a constant source of encouragement to us. We ask for permission to translate *Trust God for Your Finances*. This book is badly needed by the people in Turkey." (This permission was granted.) (Turkey)

- "My mom is 95 years old. She was in the Bergen-Belsen Concentration Camp in Germany from 1943 to 1945. She has always had a lot of worry and fear. My mother was helped greatly in overcoming this problem by your Scripture cards titled *Freedom from Worry and Fear*. She was helped so much that she asked me to order another set to give to a friend." (California)

- "I am overwhelmed about the revelations in your Scripture Meditation Cards. These Scripture cards have helped me so much that

I cannot write enough on this sheet of paper. We have gone through a five-day programme in our church using the Scripture cards. My faith has increased tremendously. I no longer am submitting to my own will and desires, but I am now submitting to the will of God and it is so fantastic. God bless you, Jack and Judy Hartman." (Ghana)

- "I am very enthusiastic about your Scripture cards and your tape titled *Receive Healing from the Lord*. I love your tape. The clarity of your voice and your sincerity and compassion will encourage sick people. They can listen to this tape throughout the day, before they go to sleep at night, while they are driving to the doctor's office, in the hospital, etc. The tape is filled with Scripture and many good comments on Scripture. This cassette tape and your Scripture cards on healing are powerful tools that will help many sick people." (Tennessee) (NOTE: The ten cassette tapes for our Scripture Meditation Cards are available on 80-minute CDs as well.)

- "I meditate constantly on the healing cards and listen to your tape on healing over and over. Your voice is so soothing. You are a wonderful teacher. My faith is increasing constantly." (New Hampshire).

A Close and Intimate Relationship with God

Jack and Judy Hartman

Lamplight Ministries, Inc.

Dunedin, Florida

Copyright 2010

Jack and Judy Hartman

Jack and Judy Hartman

Lamplight Ministries Inc

PO Box 1307

Dunedin, Florida 34697-2921

Telephone: 1-800-540-1597

FAX: 1-727-784-2980

Website: lamplight.net

Email: lamplight@lamplight.net

ISBN: 978-0-915445-14-1

Library of Congress Control Number: 2010905821

Dedication

We dedicate this book to Bishop Jim Koshita Kafumukache who is a Zambian pastor and missionary to the nations. When Jim was a cell group leader in his church in 1993, his pastor gave him a copy of one of our books. Jim devoured this book and taught exclusively from it. He has immersed himself constantly in all of our books since that time. Lamplight Ministries is his Bible school.

Three years later Jim and his family moved to another area of Zambia. There was no church in this area so he started meetings in his home where people met for prayer and Bible studies every night. Soon the number of people attending could not fit in his house. Jim founded a church and ministry that was officially opened and registered in 1997. This church since has expanded into several other churches and Jim serves as bishop over these churches.

Jim has preached and taught from our books in Zambia, Tanzania, Malawi, Swaziland, Botswana and other countries in Africa. He also has conducted international crusades and conferences using our books in China, Malaysia, Belgium and the Netherlands. Jim has distributed large numbers of our books in each of these countries.

We are pleased that Jim refers to us as his spiritual parents. We are privileged to work closely on an ongoing basis with this humble and dedicated servant of God. We thank God for you, Jim. We are honored to dedicate this book to you and to every life you have touched with the ministry that God has given to you.

We each began studying the Bible in the *King James Version*. If we could write this entire book with the *King James Version*, we would. However, we want to present the reader with the best possible explanation of each verse of Scripture.

We have carefully reviewed each verse of Scripture in this book to prayerfully select the version of the Bible that we believe will help you to best understand what God is saying to you. In some cases we have used *The New International Version* (NIV) when we believe the language in this particular passage of Scripture will give you more comprehension. In other cases we have used *The Amplified Bible* (AMP) when we believe the amplification will explain more to you.

The *King James Version* (KJV) of the Bible received its name from King James who was the king of England from 1603 to 1625. King James is considered to have been one of the most intellectual and learned kings in the history of Great Britain. He is primarily remembered for authorizing the production of the *King James Version* of the Bible. This English translation from Greek and Hebrew is the most printed book in the history of the world with more than one billion copies in print.

The New International Version (NIV) is the result of the study of a group of approximately one hundred Hebrew and Greek scholars representing more than twenty denominations. This team of scholars devoted ten years to complete the NIV translation. The goal of this committee was to faithfully translate the original Greek, Hebrew and Aramaic biblical text into clearly understandable English. The NIV is the most widely purchased contemporary Bible today.

The Amplified Bible is the result of the study of a group of Bible scholars who spent a total of more than twenty thousand hours amplifying the Bible. They believe that traditional word-by-word translation often fails to reveal the shades of meaning that are part of the original Greek, Hebrew and Aramaic biblical texts.

Any amplification of the original text utilizes brackets for words that clarify the meaning and parentheses for words that contain additional phrases included in the original language. Through this amplification the reader will gain a better understanding of what Hebrew and Greek listeners instinctively understood.

TABLE OF CONTENTS

Introduction

This book will explain *exactly* what the Bible instructs you to do to develop a close and intimate relationship with God. Some Christians cannot understand how they can have an intimate relationship with God when they cannot physically see Him, hear Him or touch Him. A close relationship with God Who seems so distant does not make any sense to them.

Other Christians know about God, but they do not know Him intimately and personally. There is no relationship that you will ever have with any person, no matter how close this person may be to you, that can even remotely compare to the magnificence of a close and intimate relationship with God.

Jesus Christ shed His blood so that *you* can know God personally and intimately. Do not allow His sacrifice to be in vain. We pray that you will be determined to learn and to do exactly what God's Word instructs you to do so that you will enjoy the close relationship with God that the Bible promises to you and that God created you to have with Him.

Some Christians are overwhelmed by the magnitude of the Bible. We have done the work for you. We have carefully selected almost five hundred verses of Scripture that explain what you should do to draw closer to God. You will find that this book is written in simple and easy-to-understand language.

God's ways are very different from and very much higher than the ways of the world (see Isaiah 55:8-9). We will make some statements in this book that will not make any sense from the perspective of logical and intellectual worldly thinking. Every one of these principles will be solidly anchored on Scripture. We urge you to make the decision that, if you read something that is completely different from what you now believe, you will change your mind if you see that the principle we are explaining is solidly anchored upon God's Word.

As you read this book you will see that we use the *Amplified Bible* more than other versions. We have found that in many cases this version of the Bible gives you amplifications that contain valuable additional knowledge that is not found in other versions of the Bible. We have compared each verse of Scripture with the *King James* version, the *New International* version and *The Amplified Bible*. We then use whatever version enables us to best describe whatever principle we are explaining.

You will see that the verses from *The Amplified Bible* contain additional information that is contained within parentheses or brackets. This amplification from the original Hebrew and Greek will give you much greater understanding of the Scripture.

We recommend that you read this book with a highlighter or pen. Highlight or underline all scriptural truths that are meaningful to you. Make notes in the margins and at the top and bottom of each page on facts that you desire to retain.

If you decide to highlight or underline verses that are meaningful to you and to write notes in the margins, you will be *studying* the Bible. You then will be prepared for Scripture meditation.

God has instructed you to renew your mind by *studying* the Bible daily (see II Corinthians 4:16 and Ephesians 4:22-23). God also has instructed you to *meditate* day and night on His Word (see Joshua 1:8 and Psalm 1:2-3).

By highlighting or underlining and making personal notes as you study this Scripture, you will tailor-make this book for yourself. You will know exactly where to go to meditate so that you will consistently draw closer to God. You will have everything that you need from God's Word right in front of you to guide you in developing an intimate relationship with Him.

We know that there is some repetition in this book and that portions overlap with what we have written in other books. Our model is the Bible. God's Word is filled with repetition because God emphasizes through repetition. There is a great deal of overlapping in the Bible. Many times a passage of Scripture in one Book of the Bible is virtually identical or very similar to Scripture from another Book of the Bible.

Our goal is to give you hundreds of specific instructions from God's Word that will help you to draw closer to God. Difficult times are coming upon the world. If there ever has been a time to draw closer to God, we live in that time.

Do not miss out on the precious privilege that you have been given to draw closer to God. If you will carefully study and meditate on the Scripture references in the following chapters, we believe that your heart will sing with joy because of the constantly increasing intimacy in your personal relationship with God.

Chapter 1

God Desires an Intimate Relationship with *You*

You cannot have a close and intimate relationship with God if Jesus Christ is not your Savior. If you are not absolutely certain that Jesus is your Savior, please stop reading now and turn to the Appendix on page 225. If you obey the scriptural instructions in the Appendix, you *will* receive eternal salvation through Jesus Christ.

If you sincerely desire to have a close personal relationship with God, you can be certain that God created you to have fellowship with Him. You will give your Father great pleasure if you love Him so much that you consistently turn away from preoccupation with worldly pursuits to draw closer to Him. "Come close to God and He will come close to you..." (James 4:8 AMP)

This verse of Scripture consists of two parts – your part and God's part. God promises that He WILL come close to you. If God says that He *will* come close to you, you can be absolutely certain that He will do what He says. "...it is impossible for God to lie..." (Hebrews 6:18 NIV)

God is the epitome of integrity. There is no guarantee from any worldly source that can even remotely approach the guarantee of God standing 100% behind each and every promise He has made in the Bible.

If your Father says that He will come close to you, you can be absolutely certain that He *does* desire a deep and intimate personal relationship with you. "...Know in all your hearts and in all your souls that not one thing has failed of all the good things which the Lord your God promised concerning you. All have come to pass for you; not one thing of them has failed." (Joshua 23:14 AMP)

Personalize this promise from God Who always emphasizes through repetition. Please note that the words "you" and "your" are used *five* times in this one verse of Scripture.

Many of God's promises are conditional. God will do what He says He will do *if* you will do what He instructs you to do. You must "come close to God" on a regular and consistent basis. If you come close to God, there is no question that God will come close to you. *You decide* how close you will be to God.

Husbands and wives and parents and children are closely bonded if they consistently spend intimate time together. Your relationship with your heavenly Father is no different. He wants you to spend quality time with Him consistently.

Your loving Father does not want you, His beloved child, to have a distant relationship with Him or no relationship at all. However, He gave you freedom of choice when He created you. If God did not give you freedom of choice, you would be a robot.

If you do not make the decision to consistently draw closer to God, He will honor this decision even though He very much desires a close relationship with you. God knows that you ultimately will experience severe problems that you can only overcome if you are close to Him, but He always will honor your freedom to choose.

If you reach out today to draw closer to God, you will find that He is always available to communicate with you. If you continue to reach out to Him tomorrow, throughout the rest of this week, next week, next month and indefinitely into the future, He will become your closest and best friend, the One you trust the most.

You have just seen that your Father definitely desires a close relationship with you. Jesus Christ also desires a close and intimate relationship with you. Jesus said, "Behold, I stand at the door and knock; if anyone hears and listens to and heeds My voice and opens the door, I will come in to him..." (Revelation 3:20 AMP)

The words "I will come in to him" are very similar to God's promise in James 4:8. God has promised that He will come close to you. Jesus has promised that He *will* come to you.

Jesus is knocking at the door of your life. He is initiating the contact. Are you listening? Will you respond? Will you open the door? If you open the door, He will come in.

Many people have attended church regularly for many years without having a personal relationship with God. The Bible says that church attendance is important (see Hebrews 10:25). However, you must understand that your Father wants more from you than meeting with other believers on a regular basis.

God placed a desire for a close relationship with Him in the heart of every person He created. Most people enjoy going to lakes, oceans and mountains. These beautiful places are created by God. These people instinctively want to draw close to God by enjoying the grandeur of places He created.

We are not saying that you should not go to lakes, oceans, mountains and other beautiful creations of God. However, you must understand that going to these scenic places is not necessary to draw close to God. Your Father has given you the opportunity to experience His majestic presence at any time and in any place.

If you sincerely desire an intimate relationship with God, you will consistently turn away from worldly desires. Jesus said, "Whoever finds his [lower] life will lose it [the higher life], and whoever loses his [lower] life on My account will find it [the higher life]." (Matthew 10:39 AMP)

A higher life *is* available to you. This life revolves around a close and intimate relationship with God. You must turn away from the lower life of pursuing carnal desires to find the higher life of a personal relationship with God. "...the person who is united to the Lord becomes one spirit with Him." (I Corinthians 6:17 AMP)

As you continually draw closer to God, you will think, talk and act more and more the way that He thinks, talks and acts. Your relationship with God will develop consistently over a period of weeks, months and years if you consistently do what His Word instructs you to do to know Him deeply and personally.

Developing an intimate relationship with God can be compared to climbing a mountain. The higher you climb, the more you can see. If you consistently draw closer to God, you will experience an incredible relationship that you could not otherwise experience.

Your heart will sing with joy if you consistently draw closer to God. "...let him who glories glory in this: that he understands and knows Me [personally and practically, directly discerning and recognizing My character], that I am the Lord, Who practices loving-kindness, judgment, and righteousness in the earth, for in these things I delight, says the Lord." (Jeremiah 9:24 AMP)

You will rejoice as you consistently develop a more intimate relationship with God. Your Father will be absolutely delighted if you consistently turn away from the world to spend quality time to drawing closer to Him.

This first chapter proves that God *does* want a close and intimate relationship with *you*. The remainder of this book is filled with specific instructions from the Bible that will tell you exactly what your Father instructs you to do to draw closer to Him. As you taste of the wonderful intimacy of a close personal relationship with God, you will yearn for more intimacy with Him.

Now that you know that God definitely desires a close and intimate relationship with you, the time is here to do exactly what your Father instructs you to do to draw closer to Him. We pray that you will yearn so deeply for an intimate relationship with God that you will be determined to learn and obey each of these instructions. If you do, you will experience the greatest possible relationship that any person on earth can possibly experience – a deep and intimate relationship with God Himself.

Chapter 2

Jesus Christ Enables You to Come Close to God

You might wonder why the God of the universe desires a close and intimate relationship with you with all of your faults and short-comings. The psalmist asked this question when he said, "When I view and consider Your heavens, the work of Your fingers, the moon and the stars, which You have ordained and established, what is man that You are mindful of him, and the son of [earthborn] man that You care for him?"(Psalm 8:3-4 AMP)

The psalmist is talking here about the God Who created the heavens, the moon, the stars and all of the planets and galaxies in the universe and every person on earth. In this chapter we will look into the Bible for definite and specific answers to this seemingly difficult question.

You *are* unworthy of enjoying a close and intimate relationship with God. Every person on earth is separated from God because of his or her sins. "…your iniquities have separated you from your God; your sins have hidden his face from you, so that he will not hear." (Isaiah 59:2 NIV)

You can see by observing the lives of Adam and Eve before they fell that God created human beings to have a close relationship with Him. Adam and Eve enjoyed the wonderful privilege of continually being in God's presence before they sinned against God.

God told Adam that he could eat from every tree in the Garden of Eden except for one tree. "The Lord God took the man and put him in the Garden of Eden to work it and take care of it. And the LORD God commanded the man, 'You are free to eat from any tree in the garden; but you must not eat from the tree of the knowledge of good and evil, for when you eat of it you will surely die.' The LORD God said, 'It is not good for the man to be alone. I will make a helper suitable for him.'" (Genesis 2:15-18 NIV)

After giving this instruction to Adam, God created Eve to be Adam's wife. Satan then came into the picture when he tried to tempt Eve to eat the forbidden fruit. Eve told Satan that God had told her not to do this. "The woman said to the serpent, 'We may eat fruit from the trees in the garden, but God did say, 'You must not eat fruit from the tree that is in the middle of the garden, and you must not touch it, or you will die.'" (Genesis 3:2-3 NIV)

Eve obviously knew that God had forbidden her to eat this fruit. However, Satan was able to confuse Eve and to tempt her. Eve gave in to Satan's deception. "When the woman saw that the fruit of the tree was good for food and pleasing to the eye, and also desirable for gaining wisdom, she took some and ate it. She also gave some to her husband, who was with her, and he ate it." (Genesis 3:6 NIV)

Adam also disobeyed God. When Adam and Eve willfully disobeyed God's specific instructions, their relationship with God changed. "Then the man and his wife heard the sound of the LORD God as he was walking in the garden in the cool of the day, and they hid from the LORD God among the trees of the garden." (Genesis 3:8 NIV)

God was not pleased with the sin that Adam and Eve committed when they disobeyed His instructions. Please note that Adam and Eve *hid themselves* from the presence of the same God with Whom they previously had enjoyed close fellowship.

Adam and Eve experienced spiritual death when they disobeyed God. All of their descendants were born spiritually dead. *You* were born as a descendant of Adam and Eve.

Jesus Christ has intervened to prepare the way for you to draw close to God even though you were born separated from God as a descendant of Adam. If Jesus is your Savior, you are *not* spiritually dead as Adam and Eve were. Jesus has made it possible for you to fellowship with God just as Adam and Eve did in the Garden of Eden before they sinned.

Do not be concerned with your unworthiness to enjoy a close relationship with God. You have been made worthy by the blood that Jesus Christ shed for you. "...now in Christ Jesus you who once were far away have been brought near through the blood of Christ." (Ephesians 2:13 NIV)

Even though you were separated from God, you have been given the privilege of coming close to God because Jesus shed His precious blood for you on the cross at Calvary. "...a better hope is introduced, by which we draw near to God." (Hebrews 7:19 NIV)

Please note the similarity of the words "brought near" and "draw near" in these two verses of Scripture. There is no question that Jesus Christ has paid the full price for you to fellowship with God.

Even though you were far away from God before you received Jesus as your Savior, you do not have to stay far away. You now can fellowship with God just as intimately as Adam and Eve did in the Garden of Eden. Do not take this precious privilege lightly. You should be determined to learn and obey all of the specific instructions your Father has given you that will enable you to enjoy a warm and loving personal relationship with Him.

Unbelievers cannot enjoy the privilege of fellowshipping with God. All of the money in the world cannot purchase the priceless privilege of a personal relationship with God. Jesus Christ paid the full price for this precious privilege when He died for you at Calvary.

If Jesus is your Savior, you must look past your human liabilities and imperfections. This is exactly what God does. God overlooks your imperfections and shortcomings because He sees you as cleansed and pure through the blood that His beloved Son shed for you. "...the Son of God has [actually] come to this world and has given us understanding and insight [progressively] to perceive (recognize) and come to know better and more clearly Him Who is true..." (I John 5:20 AMP)

Jesus has given you the ability to progressively know God more intimately. When you do something progressively, you do it in successive steps. As you devote weeks, months and then years to pursuing a relationship with God, your relationship with Him will deepen with the passage of time.

Absolutely refuse to focus on your faults, shortcomings and imperfections. You can be certain that God is not focusing on your imperfections. Your Father yearns for a close and intimate relationship with you. "...His confidential communion and secret counsel are with the [uncompromisingly] righteous (those who are upright and in right standing with Him)." (Proverbs 3:32 AMP)

God wants to communicate on a confidential and intimate basis with each of His children. He wants to counsel you. He promises to give you these blessings if you will do your best to live an "uncompromisingly righteous" life.

You were made righteous before God through the shed blood of Jesus Christ. You live a righteous life by doing your very best to consistently learn and faithfully obey the specific instructions your Father has given you in His Book of Instructions, the Bible.

You can be certain that Jesus Christ has enabled you to enjoy a close relationship with God. "...because of our faith in Him, we dare to have the boldness (courage and confidence) of free access (an unreserved approach to God with freedom and without fear)." (Ephesians 3:12 AMP)

Do you have absolute faith that Jesus Christ has made it possible for you to approach God freely? You can approach God each day with bold faith because you are certain that Jesus has made this glorious relationship available to you. If you are absolutely certain that you have been given this privilege, your heart will overflow with joy.

Your relationship with God should not be just a Sunday morning relationship when you attend church. Your relationship with God should be deep, personal and intimate throughout every day of your life. Enjoy God every moment.

Chapter 3

Keep Your Relationship with God in First Place

Why would you ever allow anything, no matter how important it may seem, to come ahead of the magnificent privilege you have been given to constantly draw closer to God? "You are worthy, our Lord and God, to receive glory and honor and power, for you created all things, and by your will they were created and have their being." (Revelation 4:11 NIV)

Our Creator is worthy of receiving glory and honor. Nothing in the world can remotely compare to the magnificence of God. "Who among the gods is like you, O LORD ? Who is like you—majestic in holiness, awesome in glory, working wonders?" (Exodus 15:11 NIV)

Have you ever been in awe of a glorious sunrise, sunset or a beautiful place that you have seen? The same God Who creates every sunrise and every sunset and every beautiful place on earth desires an intimate relationship with you.

God is omnipotent. The word "omnipotent" means "all power." This is why He is called Almighty God. "...the Lord our God the Omnipotent (the All-Ruler) reigns!" (Revelation 19:6 AMP)

The *same* omnipotent God Who is so mighty and so powerful that He reigns over the entire universe desires a personal relationship with *you*. You should be in absolute awe that God desires an intimate relationship with you. "Oh, the depth of the riches and wisdom and knowledge of God! How unfathomable (inscrutable, unsearchable) are His judgments (His decisions)! And how untraceable (mysterious, undiscoverable) are His ways (His methods, His paths)!" (Romans 11:33 AMP)

You cannot even begin to comprehend the magnificence of God with the limitations of your human understanding. "Can you find out the deep things of God, or can you by searching find out the limits of the Almighty [explore His depths, ascend to His heights, extend to His breadths, and comprehend His infinite perfection]? His wisdom is as high as the heights of heaven! What can you do? It is deeper than Sheol (the place of the dead)! What can you know? Longer in measure [and scope] is it than the earth, and broader than the sea." (Job 11:7-9 AMP)

Jesus Christ has given you the opportunity to explore the infinite wisdom of God every day of your life. You have been given the awesome privilege of drawing closer to the Creator of the universe each day to learn from Him.

Most people cannot even begin to comprehend why God desires an intimate relationship with every person He has ever created. You have seen what the Bible says about the awesome majesty of God. You have seen that God definitely desires to have a close relationship with you.

Are you excited about this precious opportunity? You should approach God each day with a tremendous sense of humility and gratitude for the privilege you have been given.

If you have received Jesus Christ as your Savior, you can be absolutely certain that Almighty God is your loving Father and that you are His beloved child. "I will be a Father to you, and you will be my sons and daughters, says the Lord Almighty." (II Corinthians 6:18 NIV)

Jesus paid an enormous price so that you can become a member of the family of God. "…you are no longer outsiders (exiles, migrants, and aliens, excluded from the rights of citizens), but you now share citizenship with the saints (God's own people, consecrated and set apart for Himself); and you belong to God's [own] household." (Ephesians 2:19 AMP)

Every person who has not received Jesus Christ as his or her Savior is outside of God's kingdom. If you have received Jesus as your Savior, you are a member of the family of God.

The Holy Spirit Who lives in the heart of every Christian will assure you that God truly is your loving Father and that you really are His beloved child. "The Spirit Himself [thus] testifies together with our own spirit, [assuring us] that we are children of God." (Romans 8:16 AMP)

All loving parents desire an intimate relationship with each of their children. You should have a continual consciousness that God truly is your loving Father. You should yearn to draw closer to your Father, just as He yearns for a close relationship with you, His beloved child.

Do not make the mistake of thinking that God is too busy for precious quiet time with you. God is omnipresent. He is able to sit on His throne in heaven and at the same time live in the heart of every person on earth. God is able to have an intimate relationship with every one of the people He has created.

Could you pick up a telephone and call the president of the United States and immediately be invited into his or her office at the White House? Could you pick up a telephone and call the governor of your state and immediately be able to come into his or her presence? You know that you cannot do these things, but you *are* able to immediately come into the presence of the same God Who created the president of the United States, the governor of each state and every person on earth.

How many times have you called a business and heard a recorded message instead of a talking with a real person? Sometimes when you call a business you have to go through a series of recorded messages and you still cannot talk to a real person. How many times have you sat in the waiting room of a doctor, dentist or other professional and waited to see this person? You do not have to wait to see God. He is waiting for you with outstretched arms every minute of every day.

Your loving Father is delighted to spend quality time with you each day. He longs for you to turn away from people, places, things and events to consistently draw closer to Him. You must understand that you actually are ministering to God when you do this. "They shall enter into My sanctuary; and they shall come near to My table to minister to Me…" (Ezekiel 44:16 AMP)

What can you possibly do each day that can even begin to approach the importance of spending precious time alone with God? If you can comprehend the magnificence of the opportunity you have been given, you will not allow anyone or anything to come ahead of this glorious opportunity. You will carefully study and faithfully obey all of the specific instructions your Father has given that tell you how to come close to Him.

Everything in the world, no matter how attractive, is a poor substitute for a personal relationship with your loving Father. No other goal that you have can even approach the importance of continually drawing closer to God.

Jesus Christ told a parable about a man who found one of the greatest pearls he had ever seen. This man yearned to have this pearl. He sold everything he owned to buy it. Jesus said, "…the kingdom of heaven is like unto a merchant man, seeking goodly pearls: who, when he had found one pearl of great price, went and sold all that he had, and bought it." (Matthew 13:45-46 KJV)

The pearl that Jesus speaks of here is the kingdom of heaven that revolves around an intimate relationship between God and each of His children. You should be like the apostle Paul who said, "…I count everything as loss compared to the possession of the priceless privilege (the overwhelming preciousness, the surpassing worth, and supreme advantage) of knowing Christ Jesus my Lord and of progressively becoming more deeply and intimately acquainted with Him [of perceiving and recognizing and understanding Him more fully and clearly]. For His sake I have lost everything and consider it all to be mere rubbish (refuse, dregs), in order that I may win (gain) Christ (the Anointed One)," (Philippians 3:8 AMP)

Paul did not allow anything to interfere with the privilege of knowing Jesus more intimately. Paul yearned for a deeper relationship with Jesus. When a relationship develops progressively, it becomes better with the passage of time.

Paul considered everything else as "rubbish" compared to the privilege of consistently deepening his relationship with Jesus. Paul went on to say, "[For my determined purpose is] that I may know Him [that I may progressively become more deeply and intimately acquainted with Him, perceiving and recognizing and understanding the wonders of His Person more strongly and more clearly]..." (Philippians 3:10 AMP)

Paul was determined to know Jesus more intimately. Are you determined to know Jesus more intimately? Does this desire transcend everything else in your life?

What would you do if you were absolutely certain that Jesus Christ wanted to come to your home each day to visit with you? Jesus is more than willing to come to your house each and every day. He already lives there because He lives inside of you (see Galatians 2:20).

God is with you throughout every minute of every hour of every day of your life. Wherever you go, God goes with you. He said, "...I am with you and will keep (watch over you with care, take notice of) you wherever you may go..." (Genesis 28:15 AMP)

Many Christians are not continually aware of God's indwelling presence. Many Christians are busy pursuing goals that do not remotely approach the importance of spending intimate time with God. We pray that the great spiritual truths you are reading will motivate *you* to make the decision to constantly draw closer to God.

Chapter 4

Many Christians Do Not Know God Intimately

Many religious people attend church out of a sense of duty. Many Christians faithfully attend church each Sunday and possibly one or two evenings a week. They pray briefly each day. This lifestyle is good as far as it goes, but it should be only the beginning of an intense and fervent desire to draw closer to God.

Your Father wants you to be more than just a religious person. Religion is man reaching up to God. Christianity is God reaching out to you. Your Father wants every aspect of your life to revolve around Him.

Many Christians spend a few minutes in prayer each day, but they are not diligent students of the Bible (see II Timothy 2:15). They do not worship God continually as they have been instructed to do (see Psalm 113:3). They do not know and obey the many other scriptural instructions that are contained in this book. Jesus said, "...This people honoureth me with their lips, but their heart is far from me." (Mark 7:6 KJV)

These words that Jesus spoke about the Pharisees apply to many Christians. Is your heart far from the Lord? Are you continually drawing closer to God? Do you know and are you doing exactly what your Father has instructed you to develop an intimate relationship with Him?

If you truly have a close relationship with God, you will show the intimacy of this relationship by the words you speak and by your actions week after week, month after month and year after year. You will show how close you are to God by the way you react to adversity. You will show how close you are to God by the way you react to people who treat you unfairly.

Religious people do what seems right to them instead of consistently learning and doing exactly what God's Word instructs them to do (see Proverbs 14:12 and 16:25). Jesus said, "...for the sake of your tradition (the rules handed down by your forefathers), you have set aside the Word of God [depriving it of force and authority and making it of no effect]." (Matthew 15:6 AMP)

The Word of God is spiritually alive. It is filled with the supernatural power of God (see Hebrews 4:12), but you *can* make God's Word powerless and ineffective. How can you do this?

You can make the Word of God ineffective by being traditional in your thinking and doing what seems right to you instead of consistently studying and meditating on the Word of God to learn and obey your Father's specific instructions. Traditional thinking that does not line up with scriptural instructions results in a lifestyle that dilutes the supernatural power of God's Word.

Many Christians are busily engaged in worldly activities that consume a lot of their time. Many Christians are busy with Christian activities that they think will please God. God does want you to be busily engaged in Christian activities, but He wants these activities to be what He has instructed you to do because you continually hear His voice as a result of your close and intimate relationship with Him.

The following story of Jesus visiting two sisters named Martha and Mary clearly illustrates this principle. "...Jesus entered a certain village, and a woman named Martha received and welcomed Him into her house. And she had a sister named Mary, who seated herself at the Lord's feet and was listening to His teaching. But Martha [overly occupied and too busy] was distracted with much serving; and she came up to Him and said, Lord, is it nothing to You that my sister has left me to serve alone? Tell her then to help me [to lend a hand and do her part along with me]!" (Luke 10:38-40 AMP)

Martha was so busy doing what she thought she should do because Jesus was a visitor to their home that she neglected what was really important. She urged Jesus to tell Mary to help her.

The request that Martha made would seem reasonable to many people. Jesus had a different perspective. "...the Lord replied to her by saying, Martha, Martha, you are anxious and troubled about many things; there is need of only one or but a few things. Mary has chosen the good portion [that which is to her advantage], which shall not be taken away from her." (Luke 10:41-42 AMP)

Jesus pointed out what Martha (and many Christians today) should be doing. Instead of being overly busy attempting to serve God, you should consistently sit at His feet to learn from Him.

You should devote your life to activities that have eternal significance instead of focusing on endeavors that seem to be important from a worldly perspective. Jesus does not want you to be so caught up with seemingly important activities that you fail to make time first of all to sit at His feet each day and listen to Him.

Many Christians are relatively complacent. Even though difficult economic times in recent years have disturbed the apathy of some people, many Christians are still casual about God. They do not know and therefore cannot obey their Father's specific instructions to consistently draw closer to Him.

You must not allow complacency, apathy or a traditional lifestyle to block you from consistently hungering for a closer relationship with God. Lamplight Ministries gives many books to people in Third World countries. We often notice that the hunger for God is *much* greater in Third World countries than it is in North America.

Christian leaders are virtually unanimous in their opinion that we live in the last days before Jesus Christ returns. The Bible teaches that the world will experience great adversity during this time. "...in the last days will come (set in) perilous times of great stress and trouble [hard to deal with and hard to bear]." (II Timothy 3:1 AMP)

There is no question that difficult times are coming upon us. We do not know when this adversity will come, but we do know that severe adversity is coming. Adversity already has arrived for some people.

If there ever has been a time to make the quality decision to continually draw closer to God, we live in that time. Only Christians who have a close, intimate and trusting relationship with God will be able to cope with the adversity that will occur in the not-too-distant future.

Many unbelievers devote their discretionary time almost entirely to the pursuit of pleasure. Many Christians who attend church faithfully still devote a great deal of their time and energy in areas that may draw them away from God. Your Father wants you to draw closer to Him *now* before the difficult times that II Timothy 3:1 speaks of come upon us.

God in His wisdom often allows His children to experience adversity because He knows that this is the only way He can get their attention (see Psalm 119:71). We believe that many Christians who have little or no desire for a close relationship with God at this time *will* devote themselves to drawing closer to God because of the adversity that the world soon will experience.

God's ways are very different from our ways. Many times the adversity that seems so bad to you will turn out to be a blessing from God's perspective (see Proverbs 20:30, Ecclesiastes 7:3, Romans 5:3-4 and James 1:3-4).

Your Father wants your relationship with Him to be so close and intimate that you will trust Him completely at all times. He wants you to develop an indomitable spirit that cannot be overcome by adversity. Your Father wants you to run toward Him when you face adversity instead of running away from the problems you face to seek worldly solutions to these problems.

You will need deeply rooted faith in God to cope with the severe adversity that is coming upon the world. Jesus said, "...they have no real root in themselves, and so they endure for a little while; then when trouble or persecution arises on account of the Word, they immediately are offended (become displeased, indignant, resentful) and they stumble and fall away." (Mark 4:17 AMP)

Christians who do not have deeply rooted faith in God will not persevere with faith when they face difficult problems. Worldly sources will be ineffective during the hard times that are coming. The world says, "When the going gets tough, the tough get going." That is *not* what the Word of God says.

The Bible says that, instead of depending upon yourself, you should turn to God when you face adversity. "...we possess this precious treasure [the divine Light of the Gospel] in [frail, human] vessels of earth, that the grandeur and exceeding greatness of the power may be shown to be from God and not from ourselves." (II Corinthians 4:7 AMP)

The words "frail human vessels" in this verse of Scripture and the amplification are very important. These words do not sound in any way like the world's saying of "When the going gets tough, the tough get going."

God is the only solution to severe adversity. Your Father wants you to have such a close relationship with Him that you will trust Him completely, regardless of the seeming severity of the problems you face.

Your Father wants you to be absolutely certain that He is with you whenever you are in trouble. He wants you to have absolute faith that He will strengthen you and that He will help you. "God is our Refuge and Strength [mighty and impenetrable to temptation], a very present and well-proved help in trouble." (Psalm 46:1 AMP)

A refuge is a place of safety and security. God wants you to come into the Refuge He has provided when you are in trouble. He will strengthen you with His supernatural strength if you trust Him and stay close to Him (see Philippians 4:13).

The words "very present" in this verse of Scripture assure you that your Father is with you whenever you are in trouble. The words "well-proved help" assure you that God has repeatedly proven that He will help His beloved children when they are in trouble. Stay close to God. Have absolute faith that your loving Father will help you. Persevere in your faith in Him. Do not give up.

Instead of being a religious person who is going through the motions of playing church, you should yearn for a deep and intimate relationship with your Father. The next chapter is filled with facts about the zeal that you should have for a close and intimate relationship with God.

Chapter 5

Seek God with All Your Heart

Your Father does not want you to be lukewarm in your attitude regarding your relationship with Him. God does not reveal Himself to casual seekers. He reveals Himself to His children who *yearn* for a close and intimate relationship with Him. "...let us be zealous to know the Lord [to appreciate, give heed to, and cherish Him]...." (Hosea 6:3 AMP)

When you are zealous about something, you pursue this goal wholeheartedly. You should have deep appreciation for God. You should study diligently to learn exactly what He has instructed you to do to come close to Him. You should faithfully obey these instructions.

Your relationship with God should be more important than anything else in your life. "...you will seek Me, inquire for, and require Me [as a vital necessity] and find Me when you search for Me with all your heart. I will be found by you, says the Lord..." (Jeremiah 29:13-14 AMP)

The words "vital necessity" in the amplification of this passage of Scripture indicate that a close relationship is not optional. This relationship is absolutely essential. Your Father will reveal Himself to you *if* you "search for Him with all your heart."

You will not be disappointed if you have a deep spiritual hunger for a close and intimate relationship with God. "...He satisfies the longing soul and fills the hungry soul with good." (Psalm 107:9 AMP)

Do you long to know God intimately? Do you hunger for a close relationship with Him? If you can answer these questions affirmatively, your desire will be satisfied.

No Christian can yearn to know God and consistently follow His specific instructions for knowing Him intimately without being rewarded. He will give you meaning, satisfaction and fulfillment in your life that is far beyond anything you have ever experienced.

When God created you He placed a void in your heart that can only be filled by a close relationship with Him. Many people are aware of this void in their lives, but they do not know how to fill it. These people go to great extremes pursuing many things in the world in a vain attempt to fill this void. Only God can satisfy this deep inner longing. You should be like the psalmist who said, "My soul thirsts for God, for the living God. ...." (Psalm 42:2 NIV)

Do you thirst for a meaningful relationship with God? You should be like the psalmist David who said, "O God, You are my God, earnestly will I seek You; my inner self thirsts for You, my flesh longs and is faint for You, in a dry and weary land where no water is." (Psalm 63:1 AMP)

David spoke these words when he was in the wilderness without water. He was weary. David compared his physical yearning at that time with his deep spiritual thirst and longing for a deep and meaningful relationship with God.

Your Father wants you to have a similar yearning. "Wait and listen, everyone who is thirsty! Come to the waters; and he who has no money, come, buy and eat! Yes, come, buy [priceless, spiritual] wine and milk without money and without price [simply for the self-surrender that accepts the blessing]." (Isaiah 55:1 AMP)

If you truly are thirsty for an intimate relationship with God, you will come to Him each day and wait on Him. When you wait on God, you should expect to find Him. God will honor your commitment by giving you great revelation that no amount of money can buy. "...let everyone come who is thirsty [who is painfully conscious of his need of those things by which the soul is refreshed, supported, and strengthened]; and whoever [earnestly] desires to do it, let him come, take, appropriate, and drink the water of Life without cost." (Revelation 22:17 AMP)

Every Christian who thirsts for a deep and meaningful relationship with God should reach out to Him continually. Once again you are told that no amount of money can purchase the glory of intimacy with God.

Jesus Christ paid the price for your thirst to be satisfied. He said, "...whoever takes a drink of the water that I will give him shall never, no never, be thirsty any more. But the water that I will give him shall become a spring of water welling up (flowing, bubbling) [continually] within him unto (into, for) eternal life." (John 4:14 AMP)

You will never again be thirsty if you consistently drink of the spiritual water that Jesus will give you. There are no words in our earthly vocabulary that can describe the meaning and fulfillment you will experience if you stay close to Jesus.

Jesus wants you to consistently draw closer to Him throughout the remainder of your life on earth. He said, "Blessed and fortunate and happy and spiritually prosperous (in that state in which the born-again child of God enjoys His favor and salvation) are those who hunger and thirst for righteousness (uprightness and right standing with God), for they shall be completely satisfied!" (Matthew 5:6 AMP)

If you live a righteous life, you do your best at all times to learn and faithfully obey the instructions your Father has given to you in His Book of Instructions, the Bible. If you carefully study the scriptural instructions in this book pertaining to an intimate relationship with God and you hunger and thirst for this relationship, your search will be rewarded.

Complete fulfillment cannot be found from any worldly source. True fulfillment only can be found by consistently drawing closer to God. Every area of your life should revolve around your commitment to draw closer to God. You should be like the psalmist David who said, "My whole being follows hard after You and clings closely to You; Your right hand upholds me." (Psalm 63:8 AMP)

Your Father wants your relationship with Him to consistently widen and deepen as the months and years go by. You should cling to Him like the psalmist who said, "With my whole heart have I sought You, inquiring for and of You and yearning for You…" (Psalm 119:10 AMP)

Are you seeking God with your whole heart? *Do you* yearn for a close and intimate relationship with Him? You should be like King Hezekiah who was the king of Judah for 29 years. King Hezekiah was totally committed to "…seek his God [inquiring of and yearning for Him], he did with all his heart, and he prospered." (II Chronicles 31:21 AMP)

God will prosper you if you seek Him with all your heart. The Hebrew word "tsalach" that is translated as "prospered" here refers to much more than financial prosperity. This word means "to push forward, break out and go over." You will experience glorious new levels of meaning and fulfillment in your life if you continually press in to God.

Jesus is looking for total commitment from you. He said, "…he who does not take up his cross and follow Me [cleave steadfastly to Me, conforming wholly to My example in living and, if need be, in dying also] is not worthy of Me." (Matthew 10:38 AMP)

Jesus gave everything He had when He died for you at Calvary. He wants you to give your all in your deep desire and commitment to continually draw closer to Him.

Moses was a great man of God. One of the reasons that Moses was a magnificent leader was that he continually sought a more intimate relationship with God. Moses prayed saying, "…show me now Your way, that I may know You [progressively become more deeply and intimately acquainted with You, perceiving and recognizing and understanding more strongly and clearly] and that I may find favor in Your sight…." (Exodus 33:13 AMP)

Your relationship with God should progressively widen and deepen. When you do something progressively, you do whatever you are doing sequentially.

God wants you to come so close to Him that you actually become one with Him. He wants you to rejoice because of the opportunity He has given you to know Him with a degree of intimacy that is beyond the limitations of human comprehension. The more intimately you know God, the more intimately you will want to know Him.

Good habits are just as difficult to break as bad habits. If you develop the habit of studying God's specific instructions to draw closer to Him and you faithfully obey these instructions, you will enjoy a deep, meaningful and fulfilling relationship with Him.

Chapter 6

The Vital Necessity of Intimacy with God

Some of the scriptural truths in this chapter will be difficult for many people to digest. The Bible teaches that you should have a close and intimate relationship with members of your family and with other Christians. Nevertheless, no matter how close your relationship with any person may be, you will see that *no* human relationship should be more intimate than your relationship with God. "...so that He alone in everything and in every respect might occupy the chief place [stand first and be preeminent]." (Colossians 1:18 AMP)

You must not allow anyone or anything to come ahead of the intimacy of your relationship with God. You should be like the psalmist who said, "...I have no delight or desire on earth besides You." (Psalm 73:25 AMP)

God emphasizes through repetition. The Bible repeatedly emphasizes the importance of putting God in absolute first place in your life. "Seek the Lord [inquire for Him, inquire of Him, and require Him as the foremost necessity of your life]..." (Zephaniah 2:3 AMP)

The words "foremost necessity" in the amplification of this verse of Scripture are strong words. When something is foremost, nothing comes ahead of it. Once again you are told that an intimate relationship with God is a vital necessity. The psalmist David said, "You have said, Seek My face [inquire for and require My presence as your vital need]. My heart says to You, Your face (Your presence), Lord, will I seek, inquire for, and require [of necessity and on the authority of Your Word]." (Psalm 27:8 AMP)

David was determined to do exactly what the Word of God instructed him to do to come into the presence of God. Is coming into God's presence a *vital need* in your life? "...let the hearts of those rejoice who seek and require the Lord [as their indispensable necessity]. Seek, inquire of and for the Lord, and crave Him and His strength (His might and inflexibility to temptation); seek and require His face and His presence [continually] evermore." (Psalm 105:3-4 AMP)

The words "indispensable necessity" in the amplification of this passage of Scripture are emphatic words. The Word of God repeatedly emphasizes that seeking God is very important. You are instructed to crave deep and intimate fellowship with Him.

Your Father would not have told you that you can come into His presence and remain there *continually* if you could not achieve this goal. There is no better place to be than in the presence of God. The remainder of this book is filled with scriptural instructions that will tell you exactly what God instructs you to do to achieve this glorious goal.

If Jesus Christ is your Savior, you will live in God's presence throughout eternity in heaven. You *can* learn to live in His presence continually throughout the remainder of your life on earth. "...set your mind and heart to seek (inquire of and require as your vital necessity) the Lord your God...." (I Chronicles 22:19 AMP)

The Bible compares the essential need of a close relationship with God with the necessity you have to eat wholesome food. God said, "...Seek Me [inquire for and of Me and require Me as you require food]..." (Amos 5:4 AMP)

All human beings understand the importance of food for their bodies. You cannot live long if you do not eat. You can fast and you can eat lightly, but you cannot go without food for a sustained period of time.

The following advice that King David gave to his son Solomon applies to you. David said, "And you, Solomon my son, know the God of your father [have personal knowledge of Him, be acquainted with, and understand Him; appreciate, heed, and cherish Him] and serve Him with a blameless heart and a willing mind. For the Lord searches all hearts and minds and understands all the wanderings of the thoughts. If you seek Him [inquiring for and of Him and requiring Him as your first and vital necessity] you will find Him..." (I Chronicles 28:9 AMP)

God is omniscient. He knows every hair on the head of every one of the billions of people on earth (see Matthew 10:30). He knows every minute detail about each person He has created (see Psalm 139:1-4 and Hebrews 4:13). God knows exactly how much you desire to have an intimate relationship with Him. If your heart continually yearns to know God, you *will* find Him.

Can there be any question after reading the scriptural truths in this chapter that you should put your desire for a deep personal relationship with God in absolute first place in your life? If Jesus Christ is your Savior, you can be certain that God is your loving Father. You must treat the importance of your relationship with your heavenly Father more fervently than you focus on your relationship with *any* member of your human family. Jesus said, "Anyone who loves his father or mother more than me is not worthy of me; anyone who loves his son or daughter more than me is not worthy of me." (Matthew 10:37 NIV)

Your Father wants your family to be a blessing to you. He wants you to be a blessing to each member of your family. However, as much as you may love the members of your human family, Jesus emphasizes that *nothing* should come ahead of the importance of your relationship with Him.

Your relationship with your parents should not come ahead of your relationship with Jesus. Your relationship with your spouse should not come ahead of the intimacy of your relationship with Jesus. The intimacy of your relationship with your children should not come ahead of the intimacy of your relationship with Jesus. He said, "If anyone comes to Me and does not hate his [own] father and mother [in the sense of indifference to or relative disregard for them in comparison with his attitude toward God] and [likewise] his wife and children and brothers and sisters – [yes] and even his own life also – he cannot be My disciple." (Luke 14:26 AMP)

The word "hate" may seem too strong, but this word also is used in the *King James Version* and the *New International Version* of the Bible. The amplification uses the word "indifference" to describe the relative intensity of your relationship with your human family compared with the intensity of your relationship with God.

If you consistently pursue a close and intimate relationship with God ahead of everything else, you will be a *much better* husband, wife, father or mother than you will be if you allow anyone or anything to come ahead of your relationship with God. Jesus said, "I am the Vine; you are the branches. Whoever lives in Me and I in him bears much (abundant) fruit. However, apart from Me [cut off from vital union with Me] you can do nothing." (John 15:5 AMP)

Jesus is "the Vine." You are a branch of this vine. If every aspect of your life revolves around Jesus, you will produce great spiritual fruit in your life. You will become what Jesus wants you to become. You must understand that you cannot do anything that is spiritually significant if you do not have a "vital union" with Jesus Christ.

In this chapter you have repeatedly read words such as "indispensable necessity," "vital necessity" and "vital union" in the Scripture references we have studied. There is no question that God is emphasizing the absolute necessity of a close relationship with Him being in first place ahead of everyone and everything else in your life. "...you must abide in (live in, never depart from) Him [being rooted in Him, knit to Him]..." (I John 2:27 AMP)

You are told that you *must* abide in God. The amplification in this verse of Scripture says that you should "*never* depart" from Him. God uses very strong words to describe the intensity of your relationship with Him.

Your relationship with God must be deeply rooted. You should be "knit" to Him. Every aspect of your life should revolve around the intimacy of your relationship with Him. "Delight yourself also in the Lord, and He will give you the desires and secret petitions of your heart." (Psalm 37:4 AMP)

If you truly delight in God, He promises to give you the deepest desires of your heart. Your desires and His desires for you will be the *same* if you have consistent fellowship with Him. "Blessed (happy, fortunate, to be envied) are they who keep His testimonies, and who seek, inquire for and of Him and crave Him with the whole heart." (Psalm 119:2 AMP)

The words "whole heart" in this verse of Scripture mean that you should not have a half-hearted desire for a closer relationship with God. Intimacy with God should be at the top of your priority list. "...whoever would come near to God must [necessarily] believe that God exists and that He is the rewarder of those who earnestly and diligently seek Him [out]." (Hebrews 11:6 AMP)

When you do something earnestly, you are very serious and determined about what you are doing. If you seek God diligently, you will be persistent and consistent throughout every day of your life. Do these words describe *your* commitment toward seeking God?

The last three chapters have been filled with truth from the Bible pertaining to the vital importance of constantly drawing closer to God. We now are ready to look into God's Word to see *exactly* what you are instructed to do to draw closer to God throughout the remainder of your life.

Chapter 7

Turn Away from Worldly Activities

You must not make the mistake of being so occupied with worldly goals and activities that you do not set aside an ample amount of quality time to draw closer to God each day. "...beware lest thou forget the LORD..." (Deuteronomy 6:12 KJV)

These words that Moses spoke to the Israelites apply to you today. Some Christians go to church each week, pray a few minutes each day and essentially forget God during the remainder of the week. Some Christians go day after day without even thinking about God. "...My people have forgotten Me, days without number." (Jeremiah 2:32 AMP)

Please note the use of the words "forget" and "forgotten" in these two verses of Scripture. God always emphasizes through repetition. Your loving Father does *not* want you to *forget* Him. He does not want you to be a person who spends a few hours in church each week but does not have a deep desire for an intimate relationship with Him. "...You are always on their lips but far from their hearts."(Jeremiah 12:2 NIV)

When Jesus spoke to the scribes and the Pharisees, He quoted Isaiah. Jesus told these men that their religion was in form only. It was not a relationship. He said, "These people honor me with their lips, but their hearts are far from me." (Matthew 15:8 NIV)

The consistency of your thoughts, words and actions are dictated by what you truly believe in your heart. You must not be far away from Jesus in your heart. "...as he thinketh in his heart, so is he..." (Proverbs 23:7 KJV)

Most people in our generation have a much more hectic lifestyle than our parents or grandparents had. Our environment today is much busier and much noisier than when our parents and grandparents were alive.

Many people are engaged in a constant whirlwind of activity doing things that seem important to them. They allow these external activities to dominate their lives. Some Christians are so busy pursuing worldly goals that quiet time alone with God never enters their minds.

Your Father wants you to *turn away* from all of the activities, people, places, things and events that could distract you from enjoying precious quiet time alone with Him each day. He wants your value system to be the same as His value system.

Some people are caught up with a desire for worldly possessions. They spend enormous amounts of time and effort attempting to earn money over and above their needs so they can purchase things that they crave. Your Father wants you to have a sense of indifference to worldly possessions. He wants you to understand how unimportant the temporary possessions of the world are and how vitally important an intimate relationship with Him is.

In addition to pursuing wealth, some people strive to receive recognition from other people. They constantly seek to impress others. These people should be like the apostle Paul who said, "Am I now trying to win the approval of men, or of God? Or am I trying to please men? If I were still trying to please men, I would not be a servant of Christ." (Galatians 1:10 NIV)

The pursuit of pleasure rules the lives of many people today. Nowhere do we see a better example of this yearning than in the rapid growth of television during the last fifty years.

We are old enough to remember when there was no television. We remember when our parents first purchased television sets. In the early days of black and white television there were only three or four channels compared to well over one hundred channels that most people have access to today.

Television dominates the lives of many people. The latest figures from the Television Bureau of Advertising show that the average man spends four hours and thirty-five minutes watching television each day. The average woman spends five hours and fourteen minutes daily watching television. If a person works forty hours a week at his or her vocation, the thirty-plus hours that many people devote to watching television is almost equal to the time they spend earning a living.

There is nothing wrong with recreation, but recreation should not rule your life. Please stop for a moment and compare the amount of time that you watch television with the average figures you have just read. Compare the amount of time that you spend watching television each week with the quiet time that you set aside to draw closer to God.

We are not trying to condemn any person. The Bible says there is no condemnation of Christians (see Romans 8:1). We are merely trying to say that the lifestyle of many Christians today is such that they are spending *much more time* watching television and pursuing other forms of recreation than they do drawing closer to God.

Jesus Christ said that you should not be so busy that you never find time to be quiet. "The apostles [sent out as missionaries] came back and gathered together to Jesus, and told Him all that they had done and taught. And He said to them, [As for you] come away by yourselves to a deserted place, and rest a while – for many were [continually] coming and going, and they had not even leisure enough to eat. And they went away in a boat to a solitary place by themselves." (Mark 6:30-32 AMP)

Jesus said that many of His disciples were so busy with their activities as missionaries that they did not even take time to eat. This lifestyle describes the frenetic activity level of some people in our generation. You will make a big mistake if you are so busy with various activities that you do not slow down. "...his mind takes no rest even at night. This is also vanity (emptiness, falsity, and futility)!" (Ecclesiastes 2:23 AMP)

The overly active lifestyle that many people live today is vain, empty and futile. Balance is vitally important in life. You are not doing what God has called you to do if you spend too much time pursuing pleasure and if you are so busy that you do not set aside precious quality time each day to be alone with Him.

Church attendance is very important (see Hebrews 10:25). You can learn a great deal from anointed pastors and teachers. However, you cannot establish a close relationship with God through someone else. The only way that you can establish an intimate relationship with God is to set aside time each day to draw closer to Him.

The Bible emphasizes the importance of consistently drawing closer to God (see Psalm 113:3 and I Thessalonians 5:17). You cannot have an intimate relationship with God based upon the time you spent with Him last week or last month.

Many people today focus on physical fitness. Physical fitness is important, but spiritual fitness is *more* important. "...Train yourself toward godliness (piety), [keeping yourself spiritually fit]. For physical training is of some value (useful for a little), but godliness (spiritual training) is useful and of value in everything and in every way, for it holds promise for the present life and also for the life which is to come." (I Timothy 4:7-8 AMP)

Physical fitness is important during your life on earth. Spiritual fitness is eternally significant. If you continually become more spiritually fit, the great spiritual truths that you learn will bless you throughout the remainder of your life on earth and also throughout eternity. "...come out from among them, and be ye separate, saith the Lord..." (II Corinthians 6:17 KJV)

Turn away from constant preoccupation with other people. Separate yourself for daily quiet time with God. God will honor your commitment if you consistently turn away from the things of the world to draw closer to Him. "...Sanctify yourselves [that is, separate yourselves for a special holy purpose], for tomorrow the Lord will do wonders among you." (Joshua 3:5 AMP)

When you sanctify yourself, you turn away from everyone and everything else to be alone with God. If you truly desire an intimate relationship with God, you must be willing to pay a significant price.

A close relationship with God will not develop if you are passive. "...pursue that consecration and holiness without which no one will [ever] see the Lord." (Hebrews 12:14 AMP)

When you pursue something, you are very active. You go after your goal diligently. This verse of Scripture instructs you to pursue consecration. Devote yourself entirely to God.

You also are instructed to pursue holiness. Holiness is the purity of God. You should be in absolute awe of the purity of God. Your Father wants to reveal His holiness to you. You cannot experience holiness in the ways of the world.

You have a certain amount of discretionary time in your life each day. You show what your true priorities are by the way you spend this time. "Be still before the LORD, all mankind..." (Zechariah 2:13 NIV)

God is speaking to you here. He is emphasizing the importance of being still before Him. "...the Lord is in His holy temple; let all the earth hush and keep silence before Him." (Habakkuk 2:20 AMP)

God emphasizes that *everyone* should be silent before Him. You must understand the importance of consistently turning away from all external activities to be calm and quiet before God. "He makes me lie down in [fresh, tender] green pastures; He leads me beside the still and restful waters. He refreshes and restores my life (my self)..." (Psalm 23:2-3 AMP)

The beloved 23rd Psalm emphasizes the importance of lying down in green pastures and going to still and restful waters. These words apply to being still spiritually, not just going to beautiful places created by God. If you consistently spend time with God, He will refresh and restore you just as He did with David.

This chapter contains many truths from the Bible that explain the importance of turning away from worldly activities to consistently draw closer to God. In the next chapter we will study the life of Jesus during His earthly ministry to see the vital importance that Jesus placed on quiet time alone with His Father each day.

Chapter 8

Follow the Example of Jesus Christ

Jesus Christ is your example in every area of your life. If you study the accounts of His earthly ministry in the Books of Matthew, Mark, Luke and John, you will see many examples of how your Father wants you to live. Jesus spent a great deal of time alone with His Father throughout His earthly ministry.

On one occasion Jesus faced a large crowd of people who came to Him to be healed of sickness. He actually *turned away* from these people to be alone with God. "...great crowds kept coming together to hear [Him] and to be healed by Him of their infirmities. But He Himself withdrew [in retirement] to the wilderness (desert) and prayed." (Luke 5:15-16 AMP)

Can you imagine how these people must have felt when they came to Jesus expecting Him to teach them and heal them, only to see Him turn away and leave them? Jesus knew that He was unable to minister to these needy people without first spending quiet time alone with God. This same principle applies to your life today. If you sincerely desire maximum effectiveness in doing what God has called you to do with your life, you must spend a significant amount of time in His presence.

Jesus never allowed anything, no matter how important it may have seemed, to take priority over His time with God. "...it came to pass in those days, that he went out into a mountain to pray, and continued all night in prayer to God." (Luke 6:12 KJV)

Jesus spent time alone with God before He ministered to people. He also spent quiet time with God after He had ministered to many people. On one occasion after Jesus had miraculously fed five thousand men and their wives and children with only five loaves of bread and two fish, He dismissed these people. He then went up into the hills to be alone, praying to His Father. "...when he had sent the multitudes away, he went up into a mountain apart to pray: and when the evening was come, he was there alone." (Matthew 14:23 KJV)

If you study the lives of anointed and devoted Christian leaders, you will find that each of these men and women spent a considerable amount of time alone with God. These leaders were never too busy to spend time with God. Martin Luther explained this principle when he said, "I have so much to do today that I must spend several hours in prayer."

You should never be so busy that you cannot spend time with God. The busier you are, the more you need this quiet time. Do not try to find the time to be alone with God. You must *make* the time to do this.

We live in the last days before Jesus Christ will return for His church. This daily quiet time is vitally important. "Look carefully then how you walk! Live purposefully and worthily and accurately, not as the unwise and witless, but as wise (sensible, intelligent people), making the very most of the time [buying up each opportunity], because the days are evil." (Ephesians 5:15-16 AMP)

This verse of Scripture refers to our generation. You must not waste the time that God has given to you. God gives each of us twenty-four hours a day to use in whatever way we choose. Some people are so busy that they cannot comprehend how they can get quiet time with God. These people do not understand that their priorities are wrong.

Your priorities should be the same as God's priorities. You have learned that God *will* come close to you *if* you consistently reach out to Him. You should not allow business appointments, social appointments, recreational events or anything else to come ahead of the privilege you have been given to spend quality time alone with God each day. *How* can appointments with men and women take precedence over the opportunity you have been given to draw closer to God Who created each of these people?

What appointment on your daily schedule can possibly be more important than the privilege you have been given to have a daily appointment with God? Anything else that you do with your time is insignificant compared with the opportunity of spending quality time with God. Many of the problems that Christians experience come as a result of spending too much time pursuing selfish desires and too little time with God.

Check your priorities. Is God truly in first place each day of your life? Does every aspect of your daily appointment schedule come *after* your time with Him? You should not allow anyone or anything to come ahead of your daily time with God. "Thou shalt have no other gods before me."(Exodus 20:3 KJV)

Some people allow their vocation to become their god. Some people allow wealth to become their god. Some people allow the pursuit of fame to become their god. Some people allow the pursuit of pleasure to become their god. You must keep God in first place where He belongs, ahead of everything else.

Do not look at your daily schedule and think that you are too busy to find time with God. Trust God to redeem the time you spend with Him. Put your precious time with Him first each day and trust Him to cause everything else to fall into place. We have learned from many years of experience that time seems to multiply when we put God in first place where He belongs.

In addition to pursuing various worldly activities, some people spend a great deal of time each day in meaningless conversations that actually draw them away from God. "...avoid all empty (vain, useless, idle) talk, for it will lead people into more and more ungodliness." (II Timothy 2:16 AMP)

Make your words count. Use the precious privilege you have been given of vocalizing your thoughts to speak words that have eternal significance (see Matthew 12:36-37 and Ephesians 4:29).

Be very careful how you spend your time and energy. Carefully evaluate your daily activities. "...turn not aside after vain and worthless things which cannot profit or deliver you, for they are empty and futile." (I Samuel 12:21 AMP)

You must learn to discern the difference between activities that have eternal value and temporal worldly activities that have no significance in the spiritual realm. Nothing in the world, no matter how important it may seem, can even begin to compare with the eternal significance of setting aside quality time each day to be alone with God.

We have learned that giving time to God each day is similar to tithing your income to Him. When you tithe on the income you receive, you give God the first ten percent of your income. God promises you a bountiful return when you give tithes and offerings to Him. "Bring ye all the tithes into the storehouse, that there may be meat in mine house, and prove me now herewith, saith the LORD of hosts, if I will not open you the windows of heaven, and pour you out a blessing, that there shall not be room enough to receive it." (Malachi 3:10 KJV)

The same principle applies to tithing your time. If you sleep an average of seven hours a night, you are awake for seventeen hours each day. Ten percent of that is 1.7 hours a day. If you round this figure to at least two hours of daily quiet time with God, you will be tithing on your time. You can be assured that God will give you a bountiful return if you faithfully tithe on both your time and income.

Now that we have explained general principles about spending quality time alone with God each day, we will be more specific. What exactly should you do during your quiet time alone with God? You draw close to God when you pray to Him. You draw close to God when you study and meditate on His Word. You draw close to God when you learn how to hear Him speaking to you. You draw close to God when you praise Him and worship Him.

In the remainder of this book we will go into each of these and other areas to explain exactly what the Bible instructs you to do when you spend quality time alone with God each day. You do not need to spend all of your quiet time with God in an enclosed area. We have found that time spent in physical exercise often provides an opportunity for quality time with God.

I (Jack) have walked vigorously almost every day for thirty-seven years. I have found that I often hear God's voice clearly when I walk or in the relaxed time immediately after I finish exercising. I have stopped hundreds of times over the years to write notes in a small memo pad pertaining to what God has spoken to me as I exercise.

I begin my daily walking time with prayer. I then worship God when I exercise. I listen to worship music through a headset. I praise God as I walk. As I sing praises to Him, I come into His presence (see Psalm 95:1-2, 100:1-2 and 100:4).

If you spend a considerable amount of time in your car, you can use this time to draw closer to God. You can do a lot of praying while you are driving. You can meditate on Scripture while you are driving. You can listen to worship music and praise God and worship Him. Make the quality decision to change what may have been nonproductive time spiritually when you were behind the wheel of your car into precious time alone with God.

We want to emphasize that many people experience difficulty spending time alone with God when they first begin. There is a significant adjustment because this much quiet time is vastly different from the lifestyle these people have known. Be patient if you experience this initial frustration. Know that you are doing what God has called you to do. Trust Him to work everything out as you persevere.

Expect Satan's demons to do everything they can to try to put thoughts into your mind to dissuade you from spending time alone with God. The last thing that Satan and his demons want is for you to spend quality time with God each day. They will do everything they can to put thoughts into your mind to cause you to give up this goal. You probably will find that many distractions will come up during the early stages of the time you set aside to be alone with God.

Some people think that they are doing nothing when they spend time alone with God. They are so used to going and doing that they find it difficult to spend quiet time with God. The truth is that spending time alone with God could not be farther from doing nothing. You cannot spend time more beneficially than to spend quiet time alone with God each day.

Be patient. Persevere. Expect to encounter difficulties and frustrations when you first attempt to spend daily quiet time with God.

If you experience difficulty spending a prolonged period of time alone with God, start out with a few minutes each day. Gradually increase this time. As the days turn into weeks and the weeks turn into months, you will find that you have established an excellent habit that is very beneficial to you. Do *not* give up if spending time alone with God is very difficult when you first start.

We can assure you that, if you persevere, this daily quiet time with God will become extremely meaningful to you. You ultimately will find that you will look forward to this precious time each day with joy and anticipation.

The closer you draw to God, the closer you will want to draw to Him. As your relationship with God becomes more intimate, nothing will be more important to you than to continually draw closer to Him.

You might think that spending time with God is a chore during the early days and weeks when you begin this most beneficial of all habits. Just the opposite will be true if you persevere. You will find that nothing in your life is more meaningful, fulfilling and satisfying than to continually draw closer to God by spending quality time alone with Him each day.

Christians who have not experienced the joy and contentment of precious quiet time alone with God miss out on one of life's greatest blessings. Once you begin to hear the voice of God clearly, you will want to hear from Him more and more. You would not think of missing out on the wonderful quiet time you spend with Him each day.

Everything that you yearn for deep down inside of yourself can and will be experienced to the fullest if you consistently spend quality time with God. Nothing in the world can compare with the magnificent revelation and refreshing that you will receive if you consistently make the quality decision to spend quiet time with God each day.

We all know that deeply ingrained habits are difficult to break. Once again we want to emphasize that good habits are just as hard to break as bad habits. As you develop the habit of setting aside time to be alone with God over a period of weeks and months, you will establish this wonderful habit that will be a great blessing to you throughout the remainder of your life on earth.

Chapter 9

Spend Quality Time with God in the Morning

You have learned many facts from the Bible about the importance of setting aside quiet time each day to be alone with God. This quiet time can take place at different times during the day. However, you should have one specific time each day that you set aside to be with God.

The Bible emphasizes that you should spend time with God each *morning*. Jesus Christ is your example in every area. Jesus knew that He needed to spend precious quiet time with His Father each morning before He went out to minister to people. "...Jesus went to the Mount of Olives. At dawn he appeared again in the temple courts, where all the people gathered around him, and he sat down to teach them." (John 8:1-2 NIV)

This passage of Scripture tells you that Jesus went to the Mount of Olives before He returned at dawn to teach people in the temple. We are not told what Jesus did early in the morning. We believe that He spent time with His Father to prepare for the time He would teach in the temple.

Jesus was an early riser. He consistently spent quiet time with His Father before dawn. "...in the morning, long before daylight, He got up and went out to a deserted place, and there He prayed." (Mark 1:35 AMP)

Jesus arose long before the sun came up to go to a quiet place to pray. When you pray, you talk to God and you listen to Him. Jesus talked to His Father in the early morning hours. He listened to His Father in the early morning hours.

The prophet Isaiah prophesied about the earthly ministry of Jesus Christ many years before Jesus came to earth. Isaiah, speaking of Jesus, said, "…He wakens Me morning by morning, He wakens My ear to hear as a disciple [as one who is taught]." (Isaiah 50:4 AMP)

Isaiah prophesied that God would awaken Jesus each morning to teach Him. This same principle applies to your life today. If Jesus Christ is your Savior, you are a child of God. Your Father will teach you early in the morning just as He taught Jesus in the early morning hours.

The Bible says that the psalmist David also was an early riser. David said, "…I will awake right early [I will awaken the dawn]!" (Psalm 57:8 AMP)

David was awake before dawn. He prayed to God in the morning saying, "Cause me to hear Your loving-kindness in the morning, for on You do I lean and in You do I trust. Cause me to know the way wherein I should walk, for I lift up my inner self to You." (Psalm 143:8 AMP)

David knew that God loved Him. He trusted God completely. He prayed to God in the early morning hours asking Him to provide guidance for the upcoming day.

God is waiting for *you* each morning. He wants to spend quality time with you at the beginning of each day. We have previously studied the following passage of Scripture, but we want to look at it again because of the emphasis placed on God visiting with you each morning. "What is man that You should magnify him and think him important? And that You should set Your mind upon him? And that You should visit him every morning…" (Job 7:17-18 AMP)

God does not want to visit with you occasionally in the morning. He wants to visit with you *every* morning. You cannot begin each day in a better way than to spend quality time with God each morning.

Many unbelievers do not go to sleep until late at night. When people drink alcohol, take drugs or indulge in other unhealthy behavior, they usually do these things at night. Your Father wants you to be a morning person.

The apostle Paul urged the Thessalonians to be morning people. He said, "You are all sons of the light and sons of the day. We do not belong to the night or to the darkness. So then, let us not be like others, who are asleep, but let us be alert and self-controlled. For those who sleep, sleep at night, and those who get drunk, get drunk at night. But since we belong to the day, let us be self-controlled, putting on faith and love as a breastplate, and the hope of salvation as a helmet." (I Thessalonians 5:5-8 NIV)

This passage of Scripture says that Christians should not stay up late at night and get drunk. Satan often is depicted in the Bible as darkness. God often is referred to as light. Your Father wants you to belong to the day instead of being out with the night people. He wants you to begin each morning by putting on your spiritual armor so that you will be protected throughout the upcoming day (see Ephesians 6:11-17).

You cannot burn the candle at both ends. People who stay up late at night carousing or watching the late show on television do not set aside precious quiet time to be with God in the early morning hours. Satan wants you to stay up late. Most people who are influenced by Satan are night people.

The Bible specifically teaches that women should be early risers. Chapter 31 of the Book of Proverbs is primarily a definition of a virtuous woman. One of these virtues is early rising. "She rises while it is yet night and gets [spiritual] food for her household..." (Proverbs 31:15 AMP)

This verse of Scripture speaks of a woman preparing spiritual food for the members of her family. In addition to getting up early to prepare breakfast for her family, a woman also should pray for her family and strengthen herself spiritually for the upcoming day.

The psalmist David prayed to God early in the morning. David said, "In the morning You hear my voice, O Lord; in the morning I prepare [a prayer, a sacrifice] for You and watch and wait [for You to speak to my heart]." (Psalm 5:3 AMP)

David prayed to God in the morning. He waited for God to speak to him. God heard David's voice in the morning. David heard God's voice in the morning. You will be blessed if you follow David's example. "...those who seek me early and diligently shall find me." (Proverbs 8:17 AMP)

These words that Solomon spoke to his son also are God's instructions to you. When you do something diligently, you work hard at whatever you are doing. Pay the price of getting up early to seek God in the morning. He assures you that you will find Him.

If you wait to get your time with God at the end of the day when you are tired and ready to go to sleep, this time cannot begin to compare with the quality of the early morning hours when you are fresh and rested. Everything is quiet in the morning. The telephone has not started to ring. The activities of the upcoming day have not begun. There are no obstacles to distract you from drawing closer to God at the beginning of the day.

In the last chapter we compared spending time with God to tithing. When you tithe to God you are instructed to give Him the first ten percent of your income. You should not pay all of your bills and *then* give God whatever money remains. You should give God the *first* ten percent of your income (see Malachi 3:8-11).

God gave you His very best. He sent His only Son to pay the price for your sin. "...Christ (the Messiah) [is] the firstfruits..." (I Corinthians 15:23 AMP)

You should give God your very best just as God gave you His very best. You should give God the firstfruits of your time each day. If you put God first in the morning, you will be much more likely to keep Him first throughout each day.

You establish a solid foundation for the upcoming day when you spend quiet time with God during the early morning hours. What can you do during the early morning hours that is more important than spending wonderful intimate time with God?

If you spend this time with God each morning, you will build a solid foundation based on the glorious victory that Jesus won for you. You will strengthen yourself and build yourself up spiritually so that the victory of Jesus Christ will be manifested in your life throughout the upcoming day.

If you want to be calm, quiet and confident throughout the day, you should feed calm, quiet and confident thoughts from God into your spirit and your soul each morning. If you are facing a crisis, you will need even more time with God each morning to receive the strength from God that you need to overcome the problems you face (see Isaiah 40:28-31, Ephesians 6:10 and Philippians 4:13).

When you spend quality time with God in the morning, you make spiritual deposits that can be compared with making a deposit into a bank account. You then will be able to make withdrawals during the upcoming day from the deposit you made during the morning. You must build up a solid spiritual reserve to draw upon throughout each day of your life.

Many people begin their day with the bad news of the world from the newspaper, television, radio or internet. Your Father does not want you to begin your day with the overdose of bad news that the news media puts out in these last days before Jesus Christ returns for His church. You should be informed as to what is going on in the world, but only after beginning the day with the good news of the gospel that will prepare you to face the bad news of the world.

You should study and meditate on the Word of God in the early morning hours. You will energize yourself spiritually if you fill your eyes, your ears, your mind, your heart and your mouth with the holy Scriptures. You should be like the psalmist who said, "...I am awake before the cry of the watchman, that I may meditate on Your word." (Psalm 119:148 AMP)

When the psalms were written, the watchman in each city cried out early in the morning to waken the people. The psalmist awakened before the watchman to meditate on God's Word. *You* are instructed to meditate day and night on the Word of God (see Joshua 1:8 and Psalm 1:2-3). This Scripture meditation should begin early in the morning.

You also are instructed to praise God when the sun rises (see Psalm 113:3). You will be much more conscious of the presence of God during the day if you begin each morning with praise and worship. You will hear His voice more clearly when you establish a solid foundation during the early morning hours.

In addition to studying and meditating on the Word of God and praising and worshiping God early in the morning, you should pray for wisdom and guidance during the upcoming day. You should pray for other people who need prayer. The Bible instructs you to pray without ceasing (see I Thessalonians 5:17). This instruction includes the early morning hours.

If you have not been spending a significant amount of time with God in the early morning hours, your life will be transformed if you consistently give God the firstfruits of your time each day. Follow the example of Jesus Christ and the psalmist David.

This chapter is filled with instructions from God's Word about spending precious quality time with God each morning. Make the quality decision now that you will get up earlier to give God the firstfruits of your day.

In most areas of the United States, the government tells us when we should change our clocks for Daylight Savings Time by one hour in the spring and again in the fall. If the government can tell you when to get up earlier, you should do the same thing yourself. You will never be sorry if you establish a deeply ingrained habit of spending quality time with God at the beginning of each day.

Chapter 10

You Will Never Be Lonely

This chapter will be a bridge between two major topics. The first nine chapters have dealt primarily with the fact that your Father clearly instructs you to have a close and intimate relationship with Him based upon a substantial amount of quiet time alone with Him. The next several chapters will be filled with Scripture showing you that God lives in your heart if Jesus Christ is your Savior. God is with *you* throughout every minute of every hour of every day of your life.

In this chapter we will explore some facts about a Christian's need for solitude and the loneliness that some people experience when they are alone. *Solitude is the glory of being alone. Loneliness is the pain of being alone.*

When we use the word solitude here we are referring to quiet time alone with God each day. Mature Christians crave solitude. They yearn to continually draw closer to God. Christians who have spent little or no time alone with God often find that beginning daily quiet time with God is very difficult. These people often feel lonely when they are alone.

Loneliness is negative. Solitude is positive. Loneliness is bad. Solitude is good. Loneliness takes you down. Periods of solitude with God build you up. Loneliness believes that no one else cares. Solitude draws you closer to the One Who cares most.

Some people do not understand that they can be consistently alone without being lonely. Historians have noted on many occasions that most leaders throughout history spent a great deal of time alone. Many people who are very creative spend large amounts of time alone.

Some people are terrified by the thought of being alone for any length of time. They will do almost anything to fill the void that is caused by loneliness. These people cannot even begin to comprehend how they can spend time alone with God completely free from external stimulation from people, telephone conversations, television, radio or various forms of entertainment. Many people today have no concept of being quiet and still and turning away from all external sources of stimulation.

Satan and his demons understand this tendency that many people have. When Christians who have been inclined in this way attempt to spend time alone with God, Satan's demons hammer away at their minds. Some people do not stick to their sincere intentions to spend quality time alone with God because they are externally oriented. They are easy prey for the exploitation of Satan's demons.

Worldly counselors often advise lonely people to engage in activities with other people. Obeying this advice may help somewhat, but loneliness cannot be cured from external sources. Some of the loneliest people in the world are consistently engaged in temporary external activities, but they inevitably find that they are right back where they started when they return from activities with other people.

Many lonely people have found that some of the loneliest times they have experienced were times when they were engaged in superficial conversation with other people. You can be in a crowded room and still feel lonely. If you have a deep and intimate relationship with God, you will *never* be lonely because you will know that you are never alone. You constantly will be aware of God's presence.

If you are absolutely certain that God lives in your heart and if you have an intimate relationship with Him, you will never be lonely. You will not look to external sources to meet your needs.

Our generation is a restless generation. More people are focused on going places and doing things today than in any previous generation. Many people are constantly on the go. They have to be doing something continually.

Unfortunately, some Christians have picked up on this lifestyle of the world. They are constantly involved in activities that are centered around other people. If there is no place to go and nothing to do, they turn on the television, call someone on the telephone or do anything else they can think of to escape being alone with their thoughts.

In Chapter 7 we shared facts from surveys that have measured the tremendous growth in television viewing time during recent years. Television fills a vacuum in tens of millions of lives each day. Television provides instant distraction with the flick of a switch. Many people turn to television to fill the void of loneliness. An entire generation has grown up under the influence of television.

If you want to obey your Father's instructions to draw close to Him by spending quiet time alone with Him each day, you must understand that there is a great deal of difference between being alone and being lonely. You experience loneliness to the degree that you are separated from God.

Loneliness began in the Garden of Eden. Adam and Eve experienced loneliness for the first time as a result of sinning against God.

Sin always separates you from God. Pride and preoccupation with selfish desires will separate you from God. You will *not* be lonely if you consistently put God first, if you study and meditate on His Word each day, if you consistently pray and if you worship God continually.

You will not be lonely if every aspect of your life is centered around God. Jesus Christ is your example in every area of your life. Jesus often spent time alone with His Father during His earthly ministry. He had a continual consciousness of His Father's indwelling presence. Jesus said, "…He Who sent Me is ever with Me; My Father has not left Me alone…" (John 8:29 AMP)

Jesus knew that His Father lived in His heart and that He was with Him at all times. Every aspect of His life revolved around His relationship with His Father.

The Bible emphasizes through repetition. Jesus made a similar statement at a later time when He said, "…I am not alone, because the Father is with Me." (John 16:32 AMP)

Unbelievers are always alone in the spiritual realm. Christians are never alone. You will never experience loneliness if you set aside precious quiet time to be alone with God each day. You will never lack for wonderful companionship after you learn how to hear God's voice and to continually develop an intimate personal relationship with Him.

We all need companionship, but the most important companionship you will ever experience is the companionship of a deep and meaningful relationship with God. If you consistently learn and obey the scriptural instructions in this book and all that you find in the Bible, you will live in a spiritual atmosphere that is conducive to constantly drawing closer to God. You will rejoice continually because of the intimacy of your relationship with God.

We want to emphasize again that loneliness is caused by separation from God. The cure for loneliness is an intimate relationship with God. If you make a definite commitment to learn and obey the scriptural instructions for drawing closer to God, you will find that He will become your closest Companion.

Loneliness ultimately will take its toll in the life of every person who is separated from God. Unfortunately, some Christians are just as lonely as unbelievers because they have not learned and do not obey the specific instructions in the Bible that tell them how to draw closer to God.

If loneliness is a problem in your life, we believe that you will be very pleased with the scriptural content of the following chapters. You will read one scriptural fact after another that will reveal how God lives in your heart and that He is with you at all times. You cannot be lonely if you are absolutely certain Who lives inside of you.

We now are ready to carefully study God's Word to learn great spiritual truths about God being with *you* at all times.

Chapter 11

God Makes His Home in Your Heart

You have just read many scriptural truths about the vital importance of setting aside daily quiet time to fellowship with God. Some people may not comprehend this principle because they think that God sitting on His throne in heaven is so far away from them. The Bible assures you that God is *not* far away from you. "Am I a God at hand, saith the LORD, and not a God afar off?" (Jeremiah 23:23 KJV)

God could not be closer to you. If Jesus Christ is your Savior, you can be certain that the same God Who sits on His throne in heaven also lives in your heart. "One God and Father of [us] all, Who is above all [Sovereign over all], pervading all and [living] in [us] all." (Ephesians 4:6 AMP)

This verse provides assurance that God resides in the heart of every believer. The word "pervade" in this context means to be spread out throughout the world. The word "all" that is used five times in this verse of Scripture and the amplification includes you if you have asked Jesus Christ to be your Savior.

God lives in the hearts of every one of His children in South America, every one of His children in North America, every one of His children in Europe and every one of His children in every other continent throughout the world. God is omnipresent. He can be with billions of people at the same time.

You must remove any previous concepts you may have had about God not being close to you. These thoughts are based on the limitations of human understanding. *Know* that your loving Father could not be closer to you. "...He is not far from each one of us. For in Him we live and move and have our being..." (Acts 17:27-28 AMP)

The words "each one of us" in this passage of Scripture include you. Your Father wants every aspect of your life to revolve around your certainty of His indwelling presence. Your life should not be centered around yourself. Every aspect of your life should be centered upon your conviction that God is with you at all times.

Turn away from the limitations of human understanding. In the next three chapters you will read many additional facts from the Bible that will reveal more scriptural truth about God living in your heart. "Anyone who confesses (acknowledges, owns) that Jesus is the Son of God, God abides (lives, makes His home) in him and he [abides, lives, makes his home] in God." (I John 4:15 AMP)

Open your mouth and boldly say, "God makes His home in *my* heart." Say it again. Say it again. *Know* that your loving Father lives in *your* heart. "...God said, I will dwell in and with and among them and will walk in and with and among them, and I will be their God, and they shall be My people." (II Corinthians 6:16 AMP)

God always emphasizes through repetition. You have just read three passages of Scripture explaining that God lives in your heart if Jesus Christ is your Savior. Your Father definitely wants to help you throughout every day of your life. "...The beloved of the Lord shall dwell in safety by Him; He covers him all the day long, and makes His dwelling between his shoulders." (Deuteronomy 33:12 AMP)

Your loving Father will keep you safe if you trust Him completely. He will protect you every day. *Why* would you ever be afraid of anything if you are absolutely certain that God is with you at all times? "...Be strong, vigorous, and very courageous. Be not afraid, neither be dismayed, for the Lord your God is with you wherever you go." (Joshua 1:9 AMP)

These words that God spoke to Joshua when he became the leader of Israel apply to you today. God promised strength to Joshua and He promises to strengthen you. Your Father does not want you to be afraid. He tells you more than three hundred times in the Bible that you should not be afraid. "...it is the Lord your God Who goes with you; He will not fail you or forsake you." (Deuteronomy 31:6 AMP)

You can be certain that your Father is with you wherever you go. He will never let you down. "...Fear not, for I have redeemed you [ransomed you by paying a price instead of leaving you captives]; I have called you by your name; you are Mine. When you pass through the waters, I will be with you, and through the rivers, they will not overwhelm you. When you walk through the fire, you will not be burned or scorched, nor will the flame kindle upon you. For I am the Lord your God..." (Isaiah 43:1-3 AMP)

Please notice that the word "through" is used three times in this passage of Scripture. You can be certain that your loving Father will bring you safely *through* adversity *if* you will persevere in your deep, strong and unwavering faith in Him.

When you face difficult problems, your Father assures you that He is with you and that He will help you. "He shall call upon Me, and I will answer him; I will be with him in trouble, I will deliver him and honor him." (Psalm 91:15 AMP)

You can be assured that God will bring you safely through adversity if you pray to Him with absolute faith that He will answer your prayer. No problem that you will ever face, no matter how difficult it may seem, is too difficult for God. "The Lord your God is in the midst of you, a Mighty One..." (Zephaniah 3:17 AMP)

The power of God that is in you is much greater than nuclear power or any other power on earth. Whenever you face a difficult challenge, you should identify continually with the indwelling presence of God instead of focusing on the seeming severity of whatever problem you face.

You have a big God living in your heart. You must not do what many people do by allowing problems to seem too large and God to seem too small. You should do just the opposite.

The more that your mouth speaks these great truths from the Word of God, the more certain you will be that God is with you and that He will help you. The Bible says that faith comes from *hearing* the Word of God (see Romans 10:17). Your faith in God will increase steadily when your ears hear your mouth continually speaking the Word of God.

Do not allow *any* problem that you face to cause you to be discouraged. The Bible explains the mighty power of God as "...the immeasurable and unlimited and surpassing greatness of His power in and for us who believe, as demonstrated in the working of His mighty strength, Which He exerted in Christ when He raised Him from the dead and seated Him at His [own] right hand in the heavenly [places]" (Ephesians 1:19-20 AMP)

The words "immeasurable and unlimited" in this passage of Scripture emphasize that God's power is infinite. We cannot begin to comprehend the magnificent power of God with the limitations of our human understanding. God's power "surpasses greatness."

The power of God is available to every one of His children who believes this great spiritual truth. The same power that God exerted when He raised Jesus Christ from the dead is in *your* heart if Jesus Christ is your Savior. Trust God completely. The Bible speaks of "...Him Who, by (in consequence of) the [action of His] power that is at work within us, is able to [carry out His purpose and] do superabundantly, far over and above all that we [dare] ask or think [infinitely beyond our highest prayers, desires, thoughts, hopes, or dreams]" (Ephesians 3:20 AMP)

You must not limit Almighty God Who knows no limits. This verse of Scripture does not just tell you that God is able to do more than you ask Him to do or more than you think He can do. There are no limits to what God can and will do on your behalf *if* you have a close personal relationship with Him and *if* you trust Him totally, completely and absolutely.

Little children are very secure when they are with their loving parents. If these children face problems that are too difficult for them to solve, they trust completely in their parents to solve these problems. Your loving Father wants you to have this same childlike trust in Him.

Have you ever seen your heart, your liver, your spleen or any other internal organs? None of us have seen these organs, but we believe that they are inside of us because medical science says they are. Xrays, ultrasounds and MRIs can show you your internal organs, but you do not need to see these organs to believe that they are in your body. This same principle applies to your certainty that God lives in your heart.

God does not live in your heart because you have earned or deserve this privilege. He lives in your heart because of His precious love, grace and mercy. God lives in your heart because Jesus Christ paid the full price to enable you to enjoy His indwelling presence.

Do you have a continual consciousness of the indwelling presence of God? You have been given the ability to receive manifestation of God's mighty power and ability at all times. Do not struggle and strain and worry. Know that your loving Father will help you.

Chapter 12

The Victorious Jesus Christ
Lives in Your Heart

You have seen that God sits on His throne in heaven and that Jesus Christ sits next to Him. You have seen that God also lives in the heart of every Christian.

Jesus is not limited to staying next to God in heaven. Jesus also comes to reside in the heart of every person who has received Him as his or her Savior. "May Christ through your faith [actually] dwell (settle down, abide, make His permanent home) in your hearts!..." (Ephesians 3:17 AMP)

You decide through your faith whether you truly believe that Jesus has come to live permanently in your heart. If Jesus is your Savior, He will live in your heart throughout the remainder of your life on earth. "All who keep His commandments [who obey His orders and follow His plan, live and continue to live, to stay and] abide in Him, and He in them. [They let Christ be a home to them and they are the home of Christ.] And by this we know and understand and have the proof that He [really] lives and makes His home in us: by the [Holy] Spirit Whom He has given us." (I John 3:24 AMP)

This verse of Scripture explains the correlation between obeying the instructions in God's Word, seeking God's will for your life and being certain that Jesus Christ really does live in your heart. If you are humble, willing and obedient, the Holy Spirit will give you deep inner certainty that Jesus Christ really does make His home in your heart.

Your Father desires an intimate relationship with you. Jesus Christ desires a close relationship with you. They could not be any closer. God the Father and God the Son live in *your* heart if Jesus Christ is your Savior.

As you grow and mature as a Christian, you will become increasingly aware that Jesus Christ lives within you. "Do you not yourselves realize and know [thoroughly by an ever-increasing experience] that Jesus Christ is in you…?" (II Corinthians 13:5 AMP)

Your life should be centered around the indwelling presence of Jesus Christ. The same Jesus Christ Who walked the shores of Galilee, performed many great miracles, died for your sins on the cross and rose from the dead lives in *your* heart.

Our generation lives in the last days before Jesus returns for His church. Jesus assured you that He will be with you until the end of the world when He said, "…I am with you all the days (perpetually, uniformly, and on every occasion), to the [very] close and consummation of the age…." (Matthew 28:20 AMP)

We believe that very difficult times will come upon the world before Jesus returns for His church. If there ever was a time when you need a close relationship with Jesus Christ, we live in that time. Jesus instructed you to focus continually on His indwelling presence when He said, "Dwell in Me, and I will dwell in you. [Live in Me, and I will live in you.]…" (John 15:4 AMP)

The apostle Paul knew that Jesus Christ lived in his heart. Paul had been beaten, tortured, stoned, cold and shipwrecked. He persevered throughout all of this adversity because of his absolute faith in Jesus Christ Who lived in his heart. Paul said, "For me to live is Christ [His life in me]…" (Philippians 1:21 AMP)

Every aspect of Paul's life revolved around his certainty that Jesus was with him at all times. Every aspect of your life should revolve around your certainty that Jesus lives in your heart.

You should have such a deep and intimate relationship with Jesus that you think what He thinks and believe what He believes. "…we have the mind of Christ (the Messiah) and do hold the thoughts (feelings and purposes) of His heart." (I Corinthians 2:16 AMP)

The New Testament is filled with facts about the tremendous miracles that Jesus performed during His earthly ministry. The same Jesus Christ Who performed these miracles lives in your heart today. "Jesus Christ is the same yesterday and today and forever." (Hebrews 13:8 NIV)

Jesus is no different today than He was throughout His earthly ministry. You can trust Him completely. "...amid all these things we are more than conquerors and gain a surpassing victory through Him Who loved us." (Romans 8:37 AMP)

You are *more* than a conqueror because of the victory that Jesus won for you. The victory that He won when He rose from the dead is so great that it *surpasses* every victory that ever has been won by anyone at any time in any place. The victory that Jesus won is so magnificent that the Bible refers to Him as the "...Lord of lords, and King of kings..." (Revelation 17:14 KJV)

If Jesus Christ is your Savior, you can be absolutely certain that the Lord of lords and King of kings lives in *your* heart. Draw closer to Jesus throughout every day of your life. Place all of your trust in Him. "...everyone born of God overcomes the world. This is the victory that has overcome the world, even our faith. Who is it that overcomes the world? Only he who believes that Jesus is the Son of God." (I John 5:4-5 NIV)

If Jesus Christ is your Savior, you have been born into God's family. You *will* overcome every obstacle that you will ever face *if* you are absolutely certain that the victorious Jesus Christ lives in you and *if* you have such an intimate relationship with Jesus that you trust Him completely. "...thanks be to God, Who in Christ always leads us in triumph [as trophies of Christ's victory]..." (II Corinthians 2:14 AMP)

The words "always leads us in triumph" apply to *every* problem you face today and *every* problem you will face throughout the remainder of your life. Meditate continually on this great promise if you are facing severe adversity. Persevere in your faith in God. Know that you will walk in victory that Jesus Christ won for you. Absolutely refuse to give up.

Jesus already has won a total victory over every problem. You should never allow anyone or anything to take precedence over "...Christ, who is your life..." (Colossians 3:4 NIV)

Every aspect of your life should be centered around your absolute certainty Jesus Christ lives in your heart. "...consider yourselves also dead to sin and your relation to it broken, but alive to God [living in unbroken fellowship with Him] in Christ Jesus." (Romans 6:11 AMP)

You should have continual intimate fellowship with your Father Who lives in your heart. You should have continual fellowship with Jesus Christ Who lives in your heart. If you have a close relationship with God and with Jesus, you will not deliberately sin. You will be so close to God and to Jesus that sin will not be able to obtain a foothold in your life.

In the last two chapters you have read many interesting truths from the Bible that assure you that God lives in your heart and that Jesus Christ lives in your heart. In the next chapter you will see many additional facts from the Bible that will show you that the Holy Spirit also lives in your heart.

Chapter 13

The Kingdom of God Is Within You

Jesus Christ began to perform tremendous miracles shortly after John the Baptist saw the Holy Spirit enter into Him (see Matthew 3:16-17). These miracles continued throughout the remainder of His earthly ministry. As Jesus approached what He knew would be His crucifixion, He told His disciples that it was *good* for them that He was going away.

This statement did not make any sense to the disciples. They could not understand how they could benefit if Jesus left them. Jesus said, "...it is profitable (good, expedient, advantageous) for you that I go away. Because if I do not go away, the Comforter (Counselor, Helper, Advocate, Intercessor, Strengthener, Standby) will not come to you [into close fellowship with you]; but if I go away, I will send Him to you [to be in close fellowship with you]." (John 16:7 AMP)

Jesus explained that the Holy Spirit would come to be with the disciples after He left. The amplification of this verse of Scripture explains the many blessings that the Holy Spirit would provide for the disciples. Jesus called the Holy Spirit "the Comforter." The amplification says that the Holy Spirit is "Counselor, Helper, Advocate, Intercessor, Strengthener, Standby."

If Jesus Christ is your Savior, you can be assured that the Holy Spirit lives in *your* heart (see Romans 8:9). He will comfort you, help you and strengthen you.

You have seen that God the Father is with you at all times (see Zephaniah 3:17). You have seen that Jesus Christ is with you at all times (see II Corinthians 13:5, Galatians 2:20, Ephesians 3:17 and I John 3:24). You can be certain that the Holy Spirit also is with you continually. "…God's Spirit has His permanent dwelling in you [to be at home in you, collectively as a church and also individually]" (I Corinthians 3:16 AMP)

The Holy Spirit can be in an infinite number of places at the same time. He lives in the heart of every Christian throughout the world. If Jesus Christ is your Savior, the Holy Spirit will live in your heart throughout the remainder of your life on earth.

Jesus previously had given His disciples important information concerning the Holy Spirit. Jesus referred to the Holy Spirit as "The Spirit of Truth, Whom the world cannot receive (welcome, take to its heart), because it does not see Him or know and recognize Him. But you know and recognize Him, for He lives with you [constantly] and will be in you." (John 14:17 AMP)

Please note that the word "you" is used three times in the final sixteen words of this verse of Scripture. These words that Jesus spoke to His disciples apply to *you*. When you see this much emphasis in such a short space, you can be certain that God wants to emphasize that the Holy Spirit lives permanently in *your* heart.

The Bible is God's Book of Instructions for you. The Holy Spirit is your teacher. He also is your guide. If you obey your Father's instructions to continually study and meditate on His Word, the Holy Spirit will reveal great spiritual truths to you. The Holy Spirit will help you when you are tempted to be afraid. God said, "…My Spirit stands and abides in the midst of you; fear not." (Haggai 2:5 AMP)

Living for God is more exhilarating than the most exciting adventure novel that has ever been written. You are filled with supernatural power because the Holy Spirit empowers you. The same Holy Spirit Who provided mighty power for Jesus throughout His earthly ministry can and will empower you today if Jesus is your Savior.

Your Father wants you to identify at all times with the indwelling presence of the Holy Spirit instead of focusing on whatever adversity you face. The Holy Spirit is always at peace regardless of the seeming severity of the problems you face. "...the mind of the [Holy] Spirit is life and [soul] peace [both now and forever]." (Romans 8:6 AMP)

Learn to listen to the Holy Spirit. Study the Bible to grow in your understanding of how the Holy Spirit operates. If you are ignorant of the power of the Holy Spirit within you, you will prevent Him from enabling you to live in the power of God. "Do not quench (suppress or subdue) the [Holy] Spirit" (I Thessalonians 5:19 AMP)

In the last three chapters you have read several verses of Scripture that show you that, if Jesus Christ is your Savior, God the Father, God the Son and God the Holy Spirit live in your heart. "...in Him the whole fullness of Deity (the Godhead) continues to dwell in bodily form [giving complete expression of the divine nature]. And you are in Him, made full and having come to fullness of life [in Christ you too are filled with the Godhead – Father, Son and Holy Spirit – and reach full spiritual stature]..." (Colossians 2:9-10 AMP)

Please do not read this passage of Scripture quickly and move on. Meditate thoroughly on the awesome truth that is contained in this passage of Scripture. The words "the Godhead" that are used twice in the amplification of this passage of Scripture refer to "Father, Son and Holy Spirit."

If Jesus Christ is your Savior, you are *filled* with mighty power. You are given the capacity to grow in your spirit every day of your life. You have spiritual power within you that is greater than nuclear power or any other power on earth. You must not allow ignorance, doubt or unbelief to block the mighty power of the Godhead from working in you, through you and for you.

Satan is the god of this world (see II Corinthians 4:4). He reigns over all unbelievers. He does not have any power over you that you do not give him (see Luke 10:19).

The Bible instructs you to turn away from the world. You do not belong to the world. Identify completely with the mighty power of the Godhead that is within you.

You may have many good friends in the world, but your Best Friend lives in your heart. "The man of many friends [a friend of all the world] will prove himself a bad friend, but there is a friend who sticks closer than a brother." (Proverbs 18:24 AMP)

You will never be lonely if you stay close to your Best Friend. If you continually draw closer to Him, you will understand that you can call on Him at any time for any reason, knowing that He is ready, willing and able to help you according to your faith in Him.

When Jesus was asked by the Pharisees when the kingdom of God would come, He said, "...The kingdom of God does not come with signs to be observed or with visible display, nor will people say, Look! Here [it is]! or, See, [it is] there! For behold, the kingdom of God is within you [in your hearts] and among you [surrounding you]." (Luke 17:20-21 AMP)

All of heaven's power is resident within you. The Pharisees demanded Jesus to tell them when the kingdom of God would come. Jesus told them that the kingdom of God is already here even though they could not see it.

The kingdom of God comes into your heart when you ask Jesus to be your Savior. The kingdom of God also surrounds you. Every aspect of the kingdom of God is here on earth.

When Jesus comes to live in your heart, you are connected to God. You have the presence of the Father, Son and Holy Spirit inside of you. You are plugged in to heaven.

The Holy Spirit within you is a comfort. The presence of God within you keeps you on course to heaven where you will live one day.

The Holy Spirit will cause you to be looking for Jesus Christ Who will appear in the air. The Holy Spirit is present to counsel you to be ready for that day. The Holy Spirit connects you with "...a kingdom that is firm and stable and cannot be shaken" (Hebrews 12:28 AMP)

Chapter 14

The Word of God Is Filled
with the Power of God

The Bible consists of sixty-six Books written by approximately forty human authors. These human authors did *not* write what they wrote from the limitations of their human understanding. "All scripture is given by inspiration of God, and is profitable for doctrine, for reproof, for correction, for instruction in righteousness: that the man of God may be perfect, thoroughly furnished unto all good works." (II Timothy 3:16-17 KJV)

Every word in the Bible is inspired by God Himself. Your Father anointed the human authors of the Bible so that you would have a supernatural Book of Instructions to guide you in every area of your life.

The Holy Spirit spoke to and through each of the human authors of the Bible. The apostle Paul said, "...we are setting these truths forth in words not taught by human wisdom but taught by the [Holy] Spirit, combining and interpreting spiritual truths with spiritual language [to those who possess the Holy Spirit]." (I Corinthians 2:13 AMP)

The words that the human authors of the Bible wrote were written through them, not by them. Every word that they wrote was inspired by the Holy Spirit. If you will obey your Father's instructions to study His Word each day and to meditate on His Word day and night, the Author of the Bible Who lives in your heart will guide you and continually draw closer to you.

Your Father wants you to approach His Word each day with absolute awe and reverence. He said, "…this is the man to whom I will look and have regard: he who is humble and of a broken or wounded spirit, and who trembles at My word and reveres My commands." (Isaiah 66:2 AMP)

Pride and the Bible do not go together. You will learn supernatural truths from the Bible if you approach God's Word each day with a humble and teachable heart. You should greatly appreciate the privilege you have been given to study God's Book of Instructions that was written by God Himself. You should revere the Word of God just as you should revere God Himself.

Nothing that the world has to offer should be more important to you than to continually learn what your Father has instructed you to learn. "Receive my instruction in preference to [striving for] silver, and knowledge rather than choice gold" (Proverbs 8:10 AMP)

This verse of Scripture compares dedication to Bible study and Scripture meditation to eagerly pursuing wealth. You should do whatever is necessary to provide for your family (see I Timothy 5:8), but you must not make the mistake that some people make of seeking wealth for selfish gain. Instead, you should use your time and energy to draw closer to God by faithfully obeying His instructions to consistently study and meditate on His Word that is filled with thousands of specific instructions and promises from Him.

The Word of God is one of the most important keys to intimacy with God. The Bible is filled with specific instructions from God that tell you exactly what to do to continually draw closer to Him.

Your Father has done His part. He has given you a Book of Instructions that is filled with great spiritual truths. You could spend every day of the remainder of your life studying the holy Bible and not even begin to learn everything that is contained in this awesome Book.

You should continually fill your mind and your heart with precious instructions and promises from God because you seek your Father with your whole being and with a deep desire to know Him intimately. You will fellowship each day with your Father if you partake of His Word. You should be like the psalmist who said, "Open my eyes, that I may behold wondrous things out of Your law. I am a stranger and a temporary resident on the earth; hide not Your commandments from me." (Psalm 119:18-19 AMP)

Pray each day asking God to give you supernatural revelation as you study and meditate on His Word. Turn away from the world. This world is not your home. Turn toward God by faithfully studying and meditating on His Word. "...the Word that God speaks is alive and full of power [making it active, operative, energizing, and effective]; it is sharper than any two-edged sword, penetrating to the dividing line of the breath of life (soul) and [the immortal] spirit, and of joints and marrow [of the deepest parts of our nature], exposing and sifting and analyzing and judging the very thoughts and purposes of the heart." (Hebrews 4:12 AMP)

The Bible is spiritually alive. The Word of God is so powerful that it is able to penetrate deep down inside of you between your soul and your spirit. The Bible is filled with the supernatural energy of God. You cannot spend your time more profitably than to consistently study and meditate on God's Word.

The Word of God should fill your eyes, your ears, your mind, your heart and your mouth throughout every day and night of your life. You should be like the apostle Paul who said, "...we also [especially] thank God continually for this, that when you received the message of God [which you heard] from us, you welcomed it not as the word of [mere] men, but as it truly is, the Word of God, which is effectually at work in you who believe [exercising its superhuman power in those who adhere to and trust in and rely on it]." (I Thessalonians 2:13 AMP)

You should thank God continually because you are absolutely certain that the Bible was written by God as He supernaturally anointed each of the human authors of the Bible. *You decide* how effective God's Word will be in your life. The Word of God will work effectively in your life in direct proportion to your faith in God and His Word. "...I commend you to the Word of His grace [to the commands and counsels and promises of His unmerited favor]. It is able to build you up and to give you [your rightful] inheritance among all God's set-apart ones (those consecrated, purified, and transformed of soul)." (Acts 20:32 AMP)

You did not earn the Word of God. You do not deserve the Word of God. Your Father has given you His Word by His grace. You can be certain that you will strengthen yourself spiritually each and every day of your life if you consistently study and meditate on God's supernatural living Word.

The Word of God is your spiritual food. You know that you should consistently feed your body with wholesome nutritious food to live a healthy and productive life. Your spiritual food is *more* important than the food you put into your mouth each day. Job said, "...I have esteemed and treasured the words of His mouth more than my necessary food." (Job 23:12 AMP)

Job understood the vital importance of consistently feeding himself with the spiritual food of God's Word. Jesus said, "...Man shall not live and be upheld and sustained by bread alone, but by every word that comes forth from the mouth of God." (Matthew 4:4 AMP)

You must understand the vital importance of continually partaking of the magnificent spiritual food that your Father has provided for you. You must feed your mind and your heart each day with supernatural spiritual food if you sincerely desire an intimate relationship with God.

The Word of God is multifaceted. You have just seen that the Word of God is your spiritual food. God's Word also is a spiritual seed. You plant spiritual seeds in your mind and your heart each day as you study and meditate on the holy Scriptures.

You will receive a magnificent spiritual harvest if you consistently plant the seed of God's Word into the spiritual soil of your mind and your heart. Jesus said, "As for what was sown on good soil, this is he who hears the Word and grasps and comprehends it; he indeed bears fruit and yields in one case a hundred times as much as was sown, in another sixty times as much, and in another thirty." (Matthew 13:23 AMP)

If you grasp and comprehend each day what your Father is telling you, you will bear enormous spiritual fruit for the kingdom of God from your Bible study and Scripture meditation. Jesus promises you a return of thirty times, sixty times or even as much as one hundred times on the time, effort and energy you invest in studying and meditating on His Word. You cannot spend your time more profitably than to faithfully obey your Father's instructions to consistently plant supernatural spiritual seeds from His Word into your mind and your heart.

This book is filled with hundreds of spiritual seeds from God's Word that explain exactly what you should do to develop and maintain a close relationship with God. You will draw closer to God if you will consistently study and meditate on these Scripture references. "Study and be eager and do your utmost to present yourself to God approved (tested by trial), a workman who has no cause to be ashamed, correctly analyzing and accurately dividing [rightly handling and skillfully teaching] the Word of Truth." (II Timothy 2:15 AMP)

Your Father wants you to present yourself to Him each day as a hard worker who has no reason to be ashamed because you are living your life in obedience to His instructions in the Bible. Make the quality decision that you will faithfully obey your Father's instructions to consistently study and meditate on His supernatural living Word.

In this chapter we have shared many verses of Scripture that explain the vital importance of consistently studying and meditating on the holy Scriptures. In the next chapter we will share with you many specific facts that will tell you *how to* effectively study and meditate on the holy Scriptures so that you will consistently develop a closer and more intimate relationship with God.

Chapter 15

Consistently Study and Meditate on the Word of God

Now that you have read these incredible truths pertaining to the divine inspiration of the Bible and the supernatural power of the living Word of God, we are ready to look into the holy Bible to see what it says about *renewing* your mind in the Word of God. "Do not be conformed to this world (this age), [fashioned after and adapted to its external, superficial customs], but be transformed (changed) by the [entire] renewal of your mind [by its new ideals and its new attitude], so that you may prove [for yourselves] what is the good and acceptable and perfect will of God, even the thing which is good and acceptable and perfect [in His sight for you]." (Romans 12:2 AMP)

This verse of Scripture instructs you to do two things – to turn away from the world and to renew your mind in God's Word. Many things in the world today are superficial with no eternal significance. Your Father instructs you to turn away from the ways of the world (see James 4:4 and I John 2:15-16).

You *will* turn away from the world if you consistently renew your mind in God's Word. When something is renewed, it is made like new. If you renew your mind in the Word of God over a period of months and years, your thinking will turn away from the superficial ways of the world. You will think more and more like God thinks. As you think more like God thinks, you will draw closer to Him.

Your thinking will be transformed if you steadily renew your mind in the Word of God. You will experience God's perfect will for your life. "...Though our outer man is [progressively] decaying and wasting away, yet our inner self is being [progressively] renewed day after day." (II Corinthians 4:16 AMP)

Your earthly body is temporary. It is decaying progressively. As you grow older in the natural realm, you must offset this regression in your body by consistently renewing your mind in the Word of God. We believe that there is a definite relationship between a long, full and healthy life and repeatedly renewing your mind in the Word of God.

The amplification of this verse of Scripture uses the word "progressively" twice. When something is done progressively, it is done in stages. How often are you instructed to renew your mind by studying God's Word? You have just seen that God instructs you to renew your mind "day after day." "...be constantly renewed in the spirit of your mind [having a fresh mental and spiritual attitude]" (Ephesians 4:23 AMP)

Your Father does not want you to renew your mind occasionally. He instructs you to renew your mind "constantly." If you do this, you will be consistently refreshed. Your life will be transformed. God said, "...I will imprint My laws upon their minds, even upon their innermost thoughts and understanding, and engrave them upon their hearts; and I will be their God, and they shall be My people." (Hebrews 8:10 AMP).

When Jesus Christ becomes your Savior, you are able to understand God's Word in a way that you could not understand it previously. Wonderful revelation awaits you *if* you will turn away from the world each day to renew your mind in God's Word. The Holy Spirit will give you revelation.

We now are ready to turn from the topic of *renewing* your mind in God's Word to the topic of *meditating* on God's Word. The following words that God spoke to Joshua when he became the leader of Israel apply to you today. God said, "This Book of the Law shall not depart out of your mouth, but you shall meditate on it day and night, that you may observe and do according to all that is written in it. For then you shall make your way prosperous, and then you shall deal wisely and have good success." (Joshua 1:8 AMP)

Please focus on the last part of this verse of Scripture first. Your loving Father wants you to be prosperous, wise and successful just as loving parents on earth want their children to be prosperous, wise and successful.

What exactly has your Father instructed you to do to become prosperous, wise and successful? He has instructed you to meditate day and night on His Word, to speak His Word continually and to learn everything you can from His Word and then to live your life in obedience to His instructions.

God has done His part. He has given instructions telling you how to be prosperous, wise and successful. *Are you* doing your part? Are you meditating day and night on the Word of God? Are you speaking God's Word continually? Are you living your life to the best of your ability in complete obedience to the instructions your Father has given to you?

Your Father emphasizes that you should renew your mind in His Word *each day* and that you should meditate *day and night* on His Word. "...his delight and desire are in the law of the Lord, and on His law (the precepts, the instructions, the teachings of God) he habitually meditates (ponders and studies) by day and by night. And he shall be like a tree firmly planted [and tended] by the streams of water, ready to bring forth its fruit in its season; its leaf also shall not fade or wither; and everything he does shall prosper [and come to maturity]." (Psalm 1:2-3 AMP)

Are you "delighted" with the Bible? *Do you* have a deep, strong and consistent desire to study God's Word each day and to meditate day and night on the holy Scriptures? This verse of Scripture uses the words "habitually" to describe Scripture meditation. You develop a habit by doing the same thing repeatedly over a sustained period of time.

Your Father wants you to form the habit of meditating day and night on His Word. If you establish this habit, you will be like a tree that is planted next to a stream of water that always brings forth fruit and never withers. Everything that you do will prosper.

Once again you can see the relationship between meditating day and night on God's Word and prospering. The Hebrew word "tsalach" that is translated as "prosper" in both Joshua 1:8 and Psalm 1:2 includes much more than financial prosperity. This Hebrew word means "to push forward, break out and go over." If you meditate day and night on God's Word, you will be moving forward in the spiritual realm. You will consistently experience a spiritual breakthrough.

A tree that is next to a stream of water always produces fruit. When there is no rain, this tree can tap into water from the stream through its deep roots.

This continual abundance is exactly what your Father promises to you if you obey His instructions to meditate day and night on His Word. Please see our books titled *How to Study the Bible*, *Exchange Your Worries for God's Perfect Peace*, *Receive Healing from the Lord* and *Victory over Adversity* for specific instructions on *how* to meditate on the Word of God.

If you meditate day and night on the holy Scriptures, you *will* prosper in every area of your life. You will draw closer to God because you will receive continual revelation from the Holy Spirit. Scripture meditation will give you supernatural wisdom for every decision you make.

The following words that King Solomon spoke to his son also are your Father's instructions to you. "My son, attend to my words; consent and submit to my sayings. Let them not depart from your sight; keep them in the center of your heart. For they are life to those who find them, healing and health to all their flesh. Keep and guard your heart with all vigilance and above all that you guard, for out of it flow the springs of life." (Proverbs 4:20-23 AMP)

Your Father wants you to pay close attention to His Word. He wants you to learn and faithfully obey the instructions He has given to you. You are told that God's Word should not depart from your sight. *If* you faithfully meditate day and night on the Word of God, you will keep God's Word at the forefront of your consciousness. God's Word will fill your heart.

There is a direct relationship between a heart that is filled with God's Word and your physical and spiritual health. You are instructed to guard your heart more than you protect anything else because your heart is the key to your life (see Proverbs 23:7). You must understand the vital importance of guarding what you allow to come into your heart. You achieve this goal by consistently filling your heart with the Word of God.

If you renew your mind in God's Word each day and if you meditate day and night on the holy Scriptures, you will constantly draw closer to your loving Father. Satan and his demons know this truth. They will do everything they can to steal the Word of God from your heart before it is able to take root. Jesus said, "While anyone is hearing the Word of the kingdom and does not grasp and comprehend it, the evil one comes and snatches away what was sown in his heart...." (Matthew 13:19 AMP)

Your heart is soil in the spiritual realm. The Word of God is a spiritual seed. If you hear an anointed preacher or teacher preaching or teaching the Word of God, Satan's demons will immediately try to steal God's Word from you before the Bible has the opportunity to take root in your heart.

If you faithfully obey your Father's instructions to renew your mind in His Word each day and to meditate day and night on His Word, you will be pouring His Word into your mind and your heart throughout every day of your life. God's Word will take root in your heart and you will constantly draw closer to Him.

When you study the Word of God, you *eat* the magnificent supernatural food that your Father has provided for you. When you meditate on the Word of God, you *chew and digest* this spiritual food. As you continually digest this food that God has provided, your heart will be filled with supernatural truth.

If your heart is filled with the Word of God, the abundance of God's Word in your heart will pour out of your mouth. Jesus said, "...out of the fullness (the overflow, the superabundance) of the heart the mouth speaks." (Matthew 12:34 AMP)

If you consistently meditate day and night on God's Word, your heart will be filled with God's Word. You will do what Joshua 1:8 instructs you to do by continually *speaking* the Word of God because God's Word that fills your heart will pour out of your mouth spontaneously.

Let us go back to Joshua 1:8 again. We will emphasize once again that God has instructed you to do three things – to *meditate* day and night on His Word, to *speak* His Word continually and to faithfully *obey* the instructions in His Word.

If you obey your Father's instructions to meditate day and night on His Word, you will program yourself to live your life the way He has instructed you to live. You will program yourself in a way that is similar to programming a computer.

This chapter is filled with spiritual truth about renewing your mind in the Word of God and meditating day and night on the holy Scriptures. In the next chapter we will look into God's Word to see the relationship that exists between developing a closer relationship with God and faithfully obeying the instructions your Father has given to you.

Chapter 16

Scripture Meditation and Intimacy with God

Obedience to God should not be a chore. You should be delighted to learn and obey the instructions your Father has given to you. You should be like the psalmist David who said, "I desire to do your will, O my God; your law is within my heart." (Psalm 40:8 NIV)

If your heart is filled with God's Word as a result of obeying your Father's instructions to meditate day and night on His Word, you will desire to do what He has called you to do with your life. You will be like the psalmist who said, "I will meditate on Your precepts and have respect to Your ways [the paths of life marked out by Your law]." (Psalm 119:15 AMP)

Some Christians merely *read* the Bible. Your Father instructs you to do more than that. You also must *study* the Bible and *meditate* on the holy Scriptures. As you study the Word of God, you renew your mind. You think more and more the way that God thinks.

God's Word and His plan will penetrate your mind and your heart. Your intellect will be enhanced beyond human understanding. You will live your life with the mind of Jesus Christ (see I Corinthians 2:16).

God reveals Himself to His children in many ways. One of the primary ways is through your consistently meditating on His Word. You will absorb and retain great spiritual truths when you meditate on God's Word. The Word of God will come alive deep down inside of you if you faithfully obey your Father's instructions to meditate day and night on His Word.

If you consistently study and meditate on the Word of God, the Author of the Bible will reveal Himself more and more to you. The Bible is the written Word of God. Jesus Christ is the living Word of God. As you consistently study and meditate on the written Word of God, you will know Jesus more intimately.

We believe that consistent Scripture meditation is the key to unlocking the Word of God. If you establish a definite pattern of daily Bible study and Scripture meditation over a period of time, you will mature to the place where you cannot get enough of God's Word. You will have learned so much and been blessed so abundantly that you will yearn for more intimate time with your Father and His supernatural living Word.

There is a definite relationship between meditating on God's Word, hearing God's voice and obeying God's instructions. "...to draw near to hear and obey is better than to give the sacrifice of fools [carelessly, irreverently] too ignorant to know that they are doing evil." (Ecclesiastes 5:1 AMP)

Your Father wants you to come close to Him so that you will be able to hear His voice and do what He tells you to do. Some Christians sin against God without realizing what they are doing because they have not learned God's instructions. *How* can you obey God's instructions if you do not even know what your Father has instructed you to do?

If you do not understand how God has instructed you to live, Satan's demons can easily pull you into spiritual darkness. However, if you faithfully learn and obey your Father's instructions, you will turn away from the darkness of Satan and come into the light of God (see Psalm 119:105).

If you love Jesus, you will want to spend time with Him and His Word. You will have a deep desire to do what He says to do. Jesus said, "The person who has My commands and keeps them is the one who [really] loves Me; and whoever [really] loves Me will be loved by My Father, and I [too] will love him and will show (reveal, manifest) Myself to him. [I will let Myself be clearly seen by him and make Myself real to him.]" (John 14:21 AMP)

You *show your love for Jesus* by doing what He instructs you to do. If you consistently obey God's instructions, the love of Jesus Christ will be manifested in your life.

Do you want to see Jesus clearly? Do you want Jesus to make Himself real to you? If you sincerely desire to receive these wonderful blessings, you will consistently study and meditate on His Word and obey His instructions.

The Bible explains the relationship between obeying God's instructions and drawing closer to Him. "...this is how we may discern [daily, by experience] that we are coming to know Him [to perceive, recognize, understand, and become better acquainted with Him]: if we keep (bear in mind, observe, practice) His teachings (precepts, commandments)." (I John 2:3 AMP)

If you faithfully do your best each day to obey God's instructions, you *will* know God more intimately. You should obey God's instructions because you love Him, not because you feel obligated to obey Him.

Your Father has given you thousands of instructions to bless you. He did not give you these instructions to penalize you. He knows that, if you learn and obey His instructions, the quality of your life will be much better than if you just do what seems right to you (see Proverbs 14:12).

Obedience to God is not drudgery. Obeying God is exciting. If you consistently learn and obey your Father's instructions, your life will be full and complete because you will be living the way your Father has instructed you to live.

If you truly love God, you will faithfully obey His instructions just as children who love their parents obey their instructions. If you consistently do your best to learn and obey God's instructions, you will not move away from Him as people do when they insist on their own way.

You must turn away from all selfish goals. You must turn away from religious doctrine that is legalistic and puts you in bondage to a form of religion without the living God. Consistently immerse yourself in the Word of God to learn how your Father instructs you to live. God will reveal to you any thoughts or habits that compromise your life and limit your ability to carry out His plan for your life.

Jesus wants you to understand the Bible. When He was walking with two men on the road to Emmaus, Jesus gave them revelation concerning the holy Scriptures. "...he opened their minds so they could understand the Scriptures." (Luke 24:45 NIV)

Jesus wants to open your mind so that you will understand God's Word. He said, "...If you abide in My word [hold fast to My teachings and live in accordance with them], you are truly My disciples. And you will know the Truth, and the Truth will set you free." (John 8:31-32 AMP)

Jesus has instructed you to abide in His Word. When you abide in His Word, you get into His Word every day and stay there. You meditate day and night on the holy Scriptures as you have been instructed to do. If you consistently live in obedience to these instructions that Jesus has given to you, you will be His disciple.

The Truth of God's Word will come alive in your heart to the degree that you meditate on the holy Scriptures and obey God's instructions. When you do, you will be set free from the problems that many people experience because of ignorance of God's instructions or disobedience to these instructions.

Sometimes people say, "The truth will set you free." This statement is true as far as it goes, but you must *know* the Truth. Only *then* will the Truth set you free.

Some of God's children experience significant problems in their lives because they have not paid the price of learning and obeying their Father's specific instructions. God said, "My people are destroyed for lack of knowledge..." (Hosea 4:6 KJV)

These words that God spoke pertaining to the Israelites also apply to you if you have received Jesus as your Savior. Satan and his demons are committed to do everything they can to *destroy* you (see John 10:10). One of the primary ways that Satan and his demons will try to destroy you is through deception. They know that you will have a distant relationship with God or no relationship at all if you do not faithfully learn and obey God's instructions.

The more you know about God's instructions and the more you live in obedience to them, the more you will be set free from the carnal influence of the world and from the attempts of Satan's demons to deceive you. "And all of us, as with unveiled face, [because we] continued to behold [in the Word of God] as in a mirror the glory of the Lord, are constantly being transfigured into His very own image in ever increasing splendor and from one degree of glory to another; [for this comes] from the Lord [Who is] the Spirit." (II Corinthians 3:18 AMP)

The Word of God is a spiritual mirror. If you consistently study and meditate on God's Word, you will see God more and more as He really is. You will see yourself as you really are. You will be transformed more and more into God's image. Your life will be full and complete because you will be living the way your Father has instructed you to live.

You should *immerse* yourself in God's Word day after day and faithfully obey your Father's instructions. "...He has bestowed on us His precious and exceedingly great promises, so that through them you may escape [by flight] from the moral decay (rottenness and corruption) that is in the world because of covetousness (lust and greed), and become sharers (partakers) of the divine nature." (II Peter 1:4 AMP)

The Word of God is precious and unique. The words "exceedingly great" means that God's Word is so awesome that it exceeds any greatness that any of us can comprehend with the limitations of our human understanding.

We live in the last days before Jesus Christ returns. The world that we live in today is filled with moral decay. Your Father wants you to be set free from this moral decay. He does not want His children to live the way that unbelievers live. Your Father does not want you to covet the things of the world. He does not want you to be lustful and greedy.

You can share in the nature of God. You can partake of the nature of God. You will become more and more like God if you consistently study and meditate on His Word and faithfully obey the specific instructions He has given to you.

This chapter is filled with truths from the holy Scriptures that explain the relationship between knowing God more intimately and consistently learning and obeying the instructions He has given to you. We now are ready to look into God's Word to learn about the relationship between steadily increasing your faith in God and knowing Him more intimately.

Chapter 17

Intimacy with God and Faith in God

You can see the relationship between intimacy and trust by thinking about the people you trust the most. Please stop for a moment and think of two or three people you trust more than anyone else. Please do not continue reading until you have identified these people.

Why do you trust these people so much? Don't you trust them because you have developed a close relationship with each of them over a period of time? The same principle applies in the spiritual realm. You can only trust God to the degree that you truly have an intimate relationship with Him.

If someone you do not know well makes a promise, you might be skeptical of this person. If someone you know and trust completely makes a promise to you, you do not doubt this person. You know that this person will do exactly what he or she has promised to do.

You undoubtedly have spent a great deal of time with the people you trust the most. This same principle applies to God. If you want to be able to trust God completely, you must invest a great deal of time to develop a close relationship with your loving Father.

You cannot trust God completely unless you stay close to Him day after day, week after week, month after month and year after year. Your faith in God is either increasing or decreasing. If you consistently draw closer to God, your faith in Him will increase steadily.

You cannot have deep faith in God if you only have a shallow relationship with Him or no relationship at all. Deep faith and a shallow relationship do not go together. You cannot expect to have deep, strong and unwavering faith in God if He is not at the center of your life. He must be in first place. Every aspect of your life must revolve around Him (see Acts 17:28).

God has bound Himself to His Word. He always does what His Word says He will do. God is totally reliable. If the Bible says that God will do something, you can be assured that He will always do it (see Joshua 23:14 and Hebrews 6:18). "...it is good for me to draw near to God; I have put my trust in the Lord God and made Him my refuge..." (Psalm 73:28 AMP)

This verse of Scripture explains the relationship between drawing near to God and putting your trust in Him. You will trust God completely and He will be your refuge if you consistently draw closer to Him.

The apostle Paul enjoyed an intimate personal relationship with Jesus. Paul trusted Jesus completely. He had absolute faith that Jesus was able to take care of everything he committed to Him. Paul said, "...I know (perceive, have knowledge of, and am acquainted with) Him Whom I have believed (adhered to and trusted in and relied on), and I am [positively] persuaded that He is able to guard and keep that which has been entrusted to me and which I have committed [to Him]..." (II Timothy 1:12 AMP)

Jesus wants you to trust Him so much that you *will* let go of every problem, give it to Him and *leave* it with Him. "Cast your burden on the Lord [releasing the weight of it] and He will sustain you; He will never allow the [consistently] righteous to be moved (made to slip, fall, or fail)." (Psalm 55:22 AMP)

Let go of the weight of every burden because you are certain that God will sustain you. If you have a close and intimate relationship with God, He will protect you. He will hold you in His arms. "The eternal God is thy refuge, and underneath are the everlasting arms..." (Deuteronomy 33:27 KJV)

Give every problem to God and leave it with Him. Refuse to take it back. Allow your Father to hold you in His everlasting arms. Trust Him completely.

If the person who is closest you makes a promise to you, you can depend on this person. No matter how dependable any person on earth may be, you can be certain that your loving Father is even more dependable. "God is faithful (reliable, trustworthy, and therefore ever true to His promise, and He can be depended on)..." (I Corinthians 1:9 AMP)

If your relationship with God is close and intimate, you will *never* doubt any of His promises. You will believe wholeheartedly that your Father *always* will do exactly what He has promised to do. "...they who know Your name [who have experience and acquaintance with Your mercy] will lean on and confidently put their trust in You, for You, Lord, have not forsaken those who seek (inquire of and for) You [on the authority of God's Word and the right of their necessity]." (Psalm 9:10 AMP)

Some people may not live up to your trust in them. You will trust God if you know Him well enough to have experienced His mercy. You will lean on God as your relationship with Him becomes more intimate.

If you have a close relationship with God that has developed over a period of time, you will not have to struggle, strain and work to have faith in Him. Deep faith in God is natural and normal for all of His children who are close to Him. Your trust in your loving Father should be spontaneous. You cannot manufacture it.

Your faith in God will increase if you obey His instructions to meditate day and night on His Word. When you meditate on God's Word, you continually *speak* the Scripture verses. Your ears will hear your mouth continually speaking the Word of God as you meditate on God's Word. "...faith cometh by hearing, and hearing by the word of God." (Romans 10:17 KJV)

Your faith in God increases when you *hear* the Word of God. Your faith in God can increase when you hear an anointed pastor or teacher preaching or teaching God's Word. However, we have learned that your faith in God will increase the most if *your* ears consistently hear *your* mouth boldly speaking God's promises as you meditate on them.

The Israelites did not receive manifestation of God's promises because they did not trust God completely. "...we have had the glad tidings [Gospel of God] proclaimed to us just as truly as they [the Israelites of old did when the good news of deliverance from bondage came to them]; but the message they heard did not benefit them, because it was not mixed with faith (with the leaning of the entire personality on God in absolute trust and confidence in His power, wisdom, and goodness) by those who heard it..." (Hebrews 4:2 AMP)

Every Christian has the same promises from God in his or her Bible. What you do with these promises determines your faith in God. Do you lean totally, completely and absolutely on God whenever you face a difficult problem? Do you have absolute trust and confidence in God at all times because you have such an intimate relationship with Him?

Only Christians who have absolute trust and confidence in God will be able to let go of seemingly unsolvable problems and give them to God and leave them with Him. "We live by faith, not by sight." (II Corinthians 5:7 NIV)

Your Father does not want your faith to be determined by what you can or cannot see. He wants you to live with absolute faith in Him regardless of external circumstances. "Though you have not seen him, you love him; and even though you do not see him now, you believe in him and are filled with an inexpressible and glorious joy," (I Peter 1:8 NIV)

You do not have to see God with your natural eyesight to have an intimate relationship with Him. You will trust God completely if you learn and faithfully obey the scriptural instructions that explain how to constantly draw closer to God. Your heart will sing with joy if you love God with all your heart, know Him intimately and trust Him completely.

Trusting God in the face of seemingly unsolvable problems can be compared to a pilot who is flying on instruments when there is no visibility. When pilots cannot see anything, they place *all* of their trust in the plane's instruments.

This same principle applies to you in the spiritual realm. Trust God completely even if you cannot see any way out of the problems you face. God can see much farther than you can see. He knows the solution to every problem. God often will reveal the solution to you progressively. Persevere in faith. Do not give up.

In this chapter we have begun to explore what the Word of God says about the relationship between knowing God intimately and trusting Him completely. In the next chapter you will learn many interesting truths from the Bible that will help you to remain quiet, calm and confident in the face of adversity because you have such a close relationship with God.

Chapter 18

Focus Continually on God

Babies trust their loving parents completely. Your Father wants you to have similar childlike trust in Him. He wants you have such a close relationship with Him that you will trust Him whenever you face a difficult challenge.

There is a definite relationship between trust in God and the Word of God. The apostle Paul in his second letter to Timothy said, "...from your childhood you have had a knowledge of and been acquainted with the sacred Writings, which are able to instruct you and give you the understanding for salvation which comes through faith in Christ Jesus [through the leaning of the entire human personality on God in Christ Jesus in absolute trust and confidence in His power, wisdom, and goodness]." (II Timothy 3:15 AMP)

Paul spoke of Timothy being acquainted with the holy Scriptures since he was a child. Ideally, all Christians should be brought up in a family where emphasis is placed upon the Bible from childhood. If this has not been the case in your life, you have a lot of Bible study and Scripture meditation to do to make up for lost time.

In this verse of Scripture Paul explains the relationship between trust in Jesus and the Word of God. How do you lean on Jesus with absolute trust in Him? You do this if you have spent many years in the Word of God increasing your faith in God. Jesus said, "Come unto me, all ye that labour and are heavy laden, and I will give you rest." (Matthew 11:28 KJV)

When you have heavy burdens, you should *come to Jesus*. Instead of struggling and straining, you should rest in Him. Give your burdens to Jesus. Do not take them back. Leave them with Him. Rest in Jesus. Trust Him completely.

You can be calm and quiet in the face of adversity if you truly are resting in Jesus. "...he who has once entered [God's] rest also has ceased from [the weariness and pain] of human labors..." (Hebrews 4:10 AMP)

This verse of Scripture explains that you can only enter God's rest to the degree that you stop trying to do everything with your own strength. If you have an intimate relationship with God, you *will* rest in Him because you trust Him completely. You will be calm, quiet and confident when you face adversity. You will be like the psalmist who said, "Be still and rest in the Lord; wait for Him and patiently lean yourself upon Him..." (Psalm 37:7 AMP)

You cannot rest in the Lord if you allow yourself to be agitated and upset by the problems you face. If you have a close relationship with God, you will be quiet and calm deep down inside of yourself because you will identify much more with Him than you do with the seeming severity of the problems you face. "Be still, and know that I am God..." (Psalm 46:10 KJV)

Once again the words "be still" are used in this verse of Scripture. Your Father does not just tell you to be still. He tells you how to be still. He tells you that you should be still *because you know that He is God*.

We recommend that you open your mouth when you face difficult problems and say the words "Be still ... Be still ... Be still ... Be still ... Be still" again and again. *Tell yourself* to be still because you trust God completely. Know that God lives in your heart and that He is with you at all times.

Trust God when you cannot see what to do. Look to Him for the next step to take. Take that step. Then look to God to show you the next step. He will lead you.

The secret to remaining calm, quiet and confident when you face a crisis is in knowing God. The more intimately you know God, the calmer you will be in the face of adversity.

Jesus explained the relationship between staying calm during adversity and trusting Him. He said, "...Do not be seized with alarm or struck with fear; simply believe [in Me as able to do this]..." (Luke 8:50 AMP)

Jesus spoke these words to a man named Jairus who had just been told that his twelve year old daughter had died. Jesus told this man that he should *not* identify with this seemingly overwhelming problem. Jesus honored the faith of Jairus when He subsequently raised his daughter from death and brought her back to life (see Luke 8:51-56).

Jesus does not want you to be fearful and alarmed when you face a problem that seems to have no solution. He wants you to have such a close relationship with Him that you will have absolute faith that He can and will bring you safely through whatever problem you face.

If you have an intimate relationship with God, your value system will not be based on the things of this world. "Let not yours be the [merely] external adorning with [elaborate] interweaving and knotting of the hair, the wearing of jewelry, or changes of clothes; but let it be the inward adorning and beauty of the hidden person of the heart, with the incorruptible and unfading charm of a gentle and peaceful spirit, which [is not anxious or wrought up, but] is very precious in the sight of God." (I Peter 3:3-4 AMP)

In this passage of Scripture God speaks to a woman telling her that she should not set her values upon her external appearance. Instead, she should build her character by filling her heart with God's Word and creating inner beauty.

Your Father repeatedly emphasizes that He wants you to be calm and quiet. He does not want you to be anxious and worried. "Acquaint now yourself with Him [agree with God and show yourself to be conformed to His will] and be at peace; by that [you shall prosper and great] good shall come to you." (Job 22:21 AMP)

How can you be tranquil when you face difficult circumstances? You will prosper and receive great blessings from God *if* you have such a close relationship with Him that you focus on Him continually instead of focusing on whatever problems you face. "You will guard him and keep him in perfect and constant peace whose mind [both its inclination and its character] is stayed on You, because he commits himself to You, leans on You, and hopes confidently in You." (Isaiah 26:3 AMP)

Your loving Father promises that He *will* guard you and keep you in perfect and constant peace regardless of the circumstances you face. God is completely reliable (see Joshua 23:14). He always does what He says He will do. God will do His part *if* you will do your part.

Your part is to keep your mind "stayed on" Him. Your part is to focus constantly on God instead of giving in to the temptation to focus on whatever problems you face. Your part is to commit yourself completely to God, to lean on and to place all of your hope and confidence in Him.

Your Father *will* guard you and keep you in perfect and constant peace *if* you refuse to focus on the seeming severity of the problems you face and instead focus continually on Him because you trust Him completely. If you truly are close to God, you will be like the apostle Paul who said, "…I have learned how to be content (satisfied to the point where I am not disturbed or disquieted) in whatever state I am." (Philippians 4:11 AMP)

Paul said that he had *learned* to be calm, quiet and confident regardless of the circumstances he faced. If Paul learned how to be this way, you can as well.

Christians who do not spend a significant amount of time alone with God each day spend most of their time in the world. Because they spend so much time in the world, they turn to worldly sources of security when they face difficult circumstances.

Worldliness blocks God from moving in your life. Nothing that the world has to offer can even begin to compare with the magnificence of a deep and intimate relationship with God. You must consistently turn away from the world to draw near to God. "Do not be conformed to this world (this age), [fashioned after and adapted to its external, superficial customs]..." (Romans 12:2 AMP)

We studied this verse of Scripture when we studied what the Bible says about renewing your mind in God's Word each day. This time we will emphasize what the first portion of this verse says about turning away from the world.

Worldly people are tied into the superficial ways of the world. Their lives revolve around the things of the world. Worldly people turn to *external* sources for security. Committed Christians turn within themselves where God lives (see Ephesians 4:6).

Some Christians trust more in the government, the economy, their employer and other worldly sources of security than they do in God. Your security should come from the inside out, not from the outside in. You cannot draw closer to God unless you consistently turn away from the ways of the world. "We know [positively] that we are of God, and the whole world [around us] is under the power of the evil one." (I John 5:19 AMP)

The words "the evil one" in this verse of Scripture refer to Satan. In our generation we have seen an increasing amount of influence from Satan and his demons. The overall content of the news in your daily newspaper today is *very* different from the news when your grandparents were your age. Satan and his demons are much more dominant today.

This verse of Scripture explains that the entire world is controlled by Satan. If you do not consistently turn away from the world to draw close to God, you will be influenced by Satan and his demons just as unbelievers are.

You must make a choice throughout every day of your life whether to consistently draw closer to God or to be primarily influenced by the world. You cannot love the things of the world and also love God. "...Do you not know that being the world's friend is being God's enemy? So whoever chooses to be a friend of the world takes his stand as an enemy of God." (James 4:4 AMP)

If you are a friend of the world, you are an enemy of God. You constantly make a choice. When you face adversity, will you turn to the world and the things of the world or will you turn to God? Only Christians who have spent significant amounts of time drawing closer to God will turn away from the world and spontaneously turn to God with absolute trust and confidence in Him.

If you have an intimate relationship with God, you *will* renew your mind in His Word each day (see II Corinthians 4:16). If you do, you will think more and more the way that God thinks. You will not be worldly in your thinking. Jesus said, "...What is highly valued among men is detestable in God's sight." (Luke 16:15 NIV)

God detests the ways of the world. Your Father does not want you to be influenced by the world. God's ways are much higher and very different from the world's ways (see Isaiah 55:8-9). As your relationship with God deepens, you will live your life on a higher plane. "Let your eyes look straight ahead, fix your gaze directly before you." (Proverbs 4:25 NIV)

You must be single-minded when you face adversity. Some Christians are double-minded when they face problems. They go back and forth from faith in God to worry, anxiety and fear. Double-minded Christians *block* God from helping them (see James 1:6-8).

Keep looking straight ahead. Refuse to look to the left or right. Keep moving forward. Do not allow any circumstances that you face to stop you from focusing on God. You should be like the psalmist who said, "Mine eyes are ever toward the LORD..." (Psalm 25:15 KJV)

Very difficult times are coming upon the world. You cannot afford not to stay close to God and to trust Him completely. "For the Lord God helps Me; therefore have I not been ashamed or confounded. Therefore have I set My face like a flint, and I know that I shall not be put to shame." (Isaiah 50:7 AMP)

This verse of Scripture consists of prophetic words that Isaiah spoke pertaining to the earthly ministry of Jesus Christ. Jesus set His face "like a flint." A flint is an extremely hard and unyielding rock. Your Father wants *you* to set your face like a flint. He wants you to focus on Him at all times and to constantly draw closer to Him.

You must not allow the problems you face to pull you away from God. "...I saw the Lord constantly before me, for He is at my right hand that I may not be shaken or overthrown or cast down [from my secure and happy state]." (Acts 2:25 AMP)

You *will* be secure and happy *if* you focus continually on God instead of focusing on whatever adversity you face. "Looking away [from all that will distract] to Jesus, Who is the Leader and the Source of our faith [giving the first incentive for our belief] and is also its Finisher [bringing it to maturity and perfection]..." (Hebrews 12:2 AMP)

Jesus Christ is the source of your faith in God. When Jesus became your Savior you were given the ability to turn away from the world and to place all of your faith in God. This chapter is filled with facts from the Word of God about focusing on God instead of focusing on the problem you face. In the next chapter we will look into God's Word for specific instructions on increasing your faith in God.

Chapter 19

Lean on God with Absolute Trust

Your Father wants you to be *so* close to Him that you will trust Him completely whenever you face problems that seem to have no solution. You should be like the psalmist who said, "He only is my Rock and my Salvation, my Defense and my Fortress, I shall not be greatly moved." (Psalm 62:2 AMP)

The psalmist speaks of trusting *only* in God, not in anyone or anything else. The psalmist made a similar statement in the same psalm when he said, "My soul, wait only upon God and silently submit to Him; for my hope and expectation are from Him." (Psalm 62:5 AMP)

God always emphasizes through repetition. Once again the word "only" is used in this verse of Scripture. If you have a close and intimate relationship with God, you will put *all* of your trust in Him. You will submit to Him because you trust Him completely. *All* of your hope will be in Him.

Every aspect of your life should revolve around your certainty that Almighty God lives in your heart and that He *is* with you at all times. "Let us all come forward and draw near with true (honest and sincere) hearts in unqualified assurance and absolute conviction engendered by faith (by that leaning of the entire human personality on God in absolute trust and confidence in His power, wisdom, and goodness)..." (Hebrews 10:22 AMP)

The word "all" in this verse of Scripture includes you. Your Father instructs you to consistently draw closer to Him. He wants you to trust Him completely. The words "unqualified assurance and absolute conviction" are very positive words. Your Father wants you to be absolutely assured that He will help you. He does not want your faith in Him to waver in the slightest, regardless of the seeming severity of any adversity you face.

You are instructed to *lean* on God. When you lean on something, you place your weight on it. Let God hold you up. Trust Him completely.

Please notice that the word "absolute" is used twice in this verse of Scripture and the amplification. When something is absolute, it is unlimited, unrestricted and unqualified – it is not dependent on anything else. Do not qualify your trust in God in any way. God is mighty and powerful. He knows the answer to every question. He is good. Focus only upon Him.

If you focus continually on God, you will not be overwhelmed when you face seemingly unsolvable problems. You will be like the psalmist David who said, "I have set the Lord continually before me; because He is at my right hand, I shall not be moved. Therefore my heart is glad and my glory [my inner self] rejoices; my body too shall rest and confidently dwell in safety" (Psalm 16:8-9 AMP)

David focused *continually* on God. He knew that God was with him at all times. He refused to be distracted by focusing on anything else. David did not allow *anything* to cause his faith in God to waver. David had a glad heart. He rejoiced deep down inside of himself regardless of the circumstances he faced. He rested in God. He was certain that God would keep him safe.

The word "therefore" in this passage of Scripture is a connecting word. This word connects what David did in focusing continually on God with having a glad heart and singing with joy. Your heart *will* sing with joy if you are so close to God that you dare to place total, complete and absolute trust in Him. "Ah, Sovereign LORD, you have made the heavens and the earth by your great power and outstretched arm. Nothing is too hard for you." (Jeremiah 32:17 NIV)

The prophet Jeremiah emphasized the same truth that you just read from the psalmist David. *No* problem that you will ever face is too difficult for the Creator of heaven and earth. If God had the power to create heaven and earth, He certainly has the power to solve whatever problem you face. *Nothing* is too difficult for God. Jesus said, "…With men it is impossible, but not with God: for with God all things are possible." (Mark 10:27 KJV)

If you consistently meditate on the Scripture references in this book about drawing closer to God, you *will* draw closer to Him. You will be certain deep down within yourself that God has the answer to every problem you have ever faced, every problem you face now and every problem you will face.

Some of God's children are overwhelmed because they are struggling and straining trying to solve problems that they cannot possibly solve with their human abilities. "[Most] blessed is the man who believes in, trusts in, and relies on the Lord, and whose hope and confidence the Lord is. For he shall be like a tree planted by the waters that spreads out its roots by the river; and it shall not see and fear when heat comes; but its leaf shall be green. It shall not be anxious and full of care in the year of drought, nor shall it cease yielding fruit." (Jeremiah 17:7-8 AMP)

You will be blessed tremendously *if* you place *all* of your hope, trust and confidence in God. The words in Jeremiah 17:8 are similar to the words in Psalm 1:3. These anointed words definitely came from God even though they were written by different human authors.

If you trust *completely* in God, you will be like a tree that is planted next to a river. This tree will *never* experience a drought. Its leaves will always be green because it can reach with its roots to obtain water from the river when rain does not come down from the sky.

You should not be worried about the problems you face. Your heart will sing with joy if you know Jesus intimately and if you trust Him completely to help you at all times. Jesus loves you with an incredible love that is beyond the limits of your human understanding (see Ephesians 3:17-19). He wants you to trust Him completely. "Be happy [in your faith] and rejoice and be glad-hearted continually (always)" (I Thessalonians 5:16 AMP)

You must not allow the problems you face to steal your joy. You should be happy at all times because you have absolute faith in God. Your Father wants your heart to constantly sing with joy regardless of the circumstances you face. Why wouldn't your heart sing with joy if your relationship with God is so deep that you have absolute faith in Him?

This book is filled with hundreds of specific scriptural instructions that tell you exactly what your Father instructs you to do to draw closer to Him. As you continually draw close to God, you will experience an increasing sense of well-being that will not be affected by any problems you face. As you draw closer to God over a period of weeks, months and years, your confidence in Him will increase steadily.

Your loving Father wants you to depend on Him completely. He wants you to know that He is with you at all times. He wants you to be certain that He will help you. You do not need anything else. God is more than enough.

Chapter 20

Receive Supernatural Strength from God

In the next two chapters we will look into the Bible for valuable information concerning the relationship between receiving strength from God and having a close relationship with Him. You will learn that, if you have an intimate relationship with God, His supernatural strength is available to you according to your faith in Him and your knowledge of the promises He has given to you.

The apostle Paul often required the strength of God during the ordeals that he experienced. On one occasion Paul was completely alone when he faced his accusers. He said, "...no one came to my support, but everyone deserted me. May it not be held against them. But the Lord stood at my side and gave me strength..." (II Timothy 4:16-17 NIV)

Can you imagine how Paul must have felt because everyone had left him? Paul was not bitter about the people who had deserted him. He asked God not to charge their desertion against them.

Paul did not depend on other people to help him through his ordeal. He trusted completely in God to stand by him and to give him the supernatural strength he needed.

Having good friends and loved ones to help you is a wonderful blessing. However, if you are completely alone and no one is on your side, you can be certain that God is with you. He will give you the strength you need. "...the Lord is faithful, and He will strengthen

[you] and set you on a firm foundation and guard you from the evil [one]." (II Thessalonians 3:3 AMP)

If Jesus Christ is your Savior, He is with you at all times. You can depend on Him. He will strengthen you if you stay close to Him and trust Him totally, completely and absolutely.

He will give you a solid foundation when you seem to be on shaky ground. Do not allow any problem you face, no matter how difficult it may seem, to discourage you. Have absolute faith that God will give you the supernatural strength you require.

Satan and his demons want you to give up. When you face adversity, they often will whisper in your ear to try to discourage you. In addition to promising to strengthen you, God also promises to guard you from what Satan is trying to do to you.

Do not allow Satan and his demons to obtain a foothold in your mind. Focus constantly on God, stay close to Him and receive supernatural strength from Him. "The Lord will give [unyielding and impenetrable] strength to His people..." (Psalm 29:11 AMP)

The word "unyielding" in the amplification of this verse of Scripture means that God will give you strength that is so great and powerful that it will *not* give in to anything. The word "impenetrable" means that no problem, no matter how difficult it may seem, can break through the supernatural strength that God will give you when you trust Him completely. "...the people who know their God shall prove themselves strong and shall stand firm and do exploits [for God]." (Daniel 11:32 AMP)

God explains here the relationship between knowing Him intimately and being able to receive His supernatural strength because of your faith and confidence in Him. If you have absolute faith that God will strengthen you, you will stand firmly against whatever problems you face. Your faith in God will not waver.

You will do great things for God because you will be doing them through His strength. You will be aware of God's supernatural power operating in your life.

Every aspect of your life should revolve around your absolute certainty that God is with you at all times and that He will strengthen you. "...be strong in the Lord [be empowered through your union with Him]; draw your strength from Him [that strength which His boundless might provides]." (Ephesians 6:10 AMP)

The words "through your union with Him" in the amplification of the verse of Scripture once again explain the relationship between a close relationship with God and receiving strength from Him. You can draw upon the strength of God that is inside of you. You can be certain that His supernatural strength is more than sufficient for any problem you will ever face.

Your Father loves you with an incredible love that is beyond the limits of your human comprehension. He does *not* want you to be afraid of anything. "...O man greatly beloved, fear not! Peace be to you! Be strong, yes, be strong..." (Daniel 10:19 AMP)

An angel spoke these words to Daniel when he faced severe adversity. These words apply to you today. *Know* that your Father loves you with incredible supernatural love. Refuse to give in to fear. You will remain in the supernatural peace of God if you consistently draw closer to Him and focus on the facts from His Word concerning His love for you.

God always emphasizes through repetition. Please note that He uses the words "be strong" two times in this verse of Scripture. Your Father is emphasizing that He wants *you* to *be strong* because you know that He loves you with supernatural love that is so great that you cannot understand the magnitude of His love with the limitations of your human understanding.

If you have a close relationship with God, you will trust Him completely when you cannot see any way out of the problems you face. You will be like the psalmist who said, "My flesh and my heart may fail, but God is the Rock and firm Strength of my heart and my Portion forever." (Psalm 73:26 AMP)

God is your solid Rock. His supernatural strength is available to you forever. You should be especially aware of God's presence and power when you feel weak. "...he said unto me, My grace is sufficient for thee: for my strength is made perfect in weakness. Most gladly therefore will I rather glory in my infirmities, that the power of Christ may rest upon me." (II Corinthians 12:9 KJV)

You can be certain that the supernatural strength of Jesus Christ is available to you. You did not earn this strength. You do not deserve this strength. This strength is available to you by God's grace which is more than sufficient to overcome any problems you face. Your Father wants you to rejoice because you know that the mighty strength and power of Jesus Christ is perfected in your human weakness when you face seemingly unsolvable problems.

Refuse to be concerned by your inadequacies. Focus continually on the supernatural strength of Jesus Christ Who lives in your heart. You should be like the apostle Paul who went on to say, "Therefore I take pleasure in infirmities, in reproaches, in necessities, in persecutions, in distresses for Christ's sake: for when I am weak, then am I strong." (II Corinthians 12:10 KJV)

Paul actually took pleasure in the adversity he faced. *Why* did he do this? Paul had this attitude because he was certain that that the supernatural strength of Jesus Christ was available to him.

The same supernatural strength is available to you if Jesus Christ is your Savior. Stay close to God. Trust Him completely. Open your mouth continually to speak boldly of His supernatural strength that is fully available to you at all times. "...let the weak say, I am strong." (Joel 3:10 KJV)

Refuse to allow your mouth to speak of your human weakness and inadequacy. Speak the Word of God in power and might. God's glory will come through you to others if you operate in His power.

This chapter is filled with facts from the Bible that will encourage you whenever you face problems that seem to have no solution. If you face severe problems, meditate constantly on these great truths and many others that you will find in the Bible.

Chapter 21

You Can Do *All* Things through the Strength of Jesus Christ

In this chapter we will continue looking into God's Word for information pertaining to His supernatural strength that is available to you if you are close to Him and trust Him completely. We will begin this chapter with a verse of Scripture that is *filled* with the power of Jesus Christ. "I have strength for all things in Christ Who empowers me [I am ready for anything and equal to anything through Him Who infuses inner strength into me; I am self-sufficient in Christ's sufficiency]." (Philippians 4:13 AMP)

The words "all things" by themselves are incomplete because you do *not* have strength for *all* things in your human abilities. However, when you add the words "in Christ Who empowers me," you can see that you *do* have strength for all things, no matter how severe the problems you face may seem.

Once again we want to say that God emphasizes through repetition. When the amplification of this verse of Scripture uses the word "anything" twice, this amplification emphasizes that there is nothing you cannot do through the strength of Jesus Christ.

No problems are too difficult for Jesus Christ. If Jesus is your Savior, He makes His home in your heart (see Ephesians 3:17). He "infuses inner strength" in you according to your faith in Him and your faith in the absolute reliability of God's Word.

The word "infuse" means "to pour into." Supernatural strength from Jesus Christ will pour out from deep down inside of yourself if you stay close to Jesus and have absolute faith in Him. The strength of Jesus Christ is available to you twenty-four hours a day throughout every day of your life. You will never face a problem that is too difficult for the victorious Jesus Christ Who lives in your heart (see John 16:33, Romans 8:37, II Corinthians 2:14 and I John 5:4-5).

Refuse to allow any problem you face, no matter how difficult this problem may seem, to overwhelm you. You should be like the psalmist who said, "My soul melteth for heaviness: strengthen thou me according unto thy word." (Psalm 119:28 KJV)

The psalmist faced such difficult problems that his soul felt like it was melting. He had such a heavy burden that he did not see how he could get through the ordeal he faced. The psalmist asked God to strengthen him according to His Word. The Word of God is spiritually alive and filled with the mighty supernatural power of God (see Hebrews 4:12).

If you faithfully obey your Father's instructions to renew your mind in His Word *every* day (see II Corinthians 4:16 and Ephesians 4:22) and to meditate day and night on His Word (see Joshua 1:8 and Psalm 1:2-3), you *will* have a close and intimate relationship with Jesus. You will be like the apostle Paul who said, "For this I labor [unto weariness], striving with all the superhuman energy which He so mightily enkindles and works within me." (Colossians 1:29 AMP)

You have just read about the supernatural strength and energy that the apostle Paul received when he was weary. If you are close to God, you can be certain that you will receive supernatural strength from God when you are weary and tired. "Hast thou not known? hast thou not heard, that the everlasting God, the LORD, the Creator of the ends of the earth, fainteth not, neither is weary? there is no searching of his understanding. He giveth power to the faint; and to them that have no might he increaseth strength. Even the youths shall faint and be weary, and the young men shall utterly fall: But they that wait upon the LORD shall renew their strength; they shall mount up with wings as eagles; they shall run, and not be weary; and they shall walk, and not faint." (Isaiah 40:28-31 KJV)

God has supernatural energy. He is never tired. He knows the answer to every problem. The same God Who never grows weary will give you supernatural strength and energy when you are weary.

His strength is so great that He can strengthen normally energetic young people who are completely fatigued. This same supernatural strength is available to you. Every person who waits upon the Lord will receive supernatural strength from God. When you wait on the Lord, you persevere with absolute faith that God will honor your faith in Him.

You have supernatural energy inside of you if Jesus Christ is your Savior. "Fear thou not; for I am with thee: be not dismayed; for I am thy God: I will strengthen thee; yea, I will help thee; yea, I will uphold thee with the right hand of my righteousness." (Isaiah 41:10 KJV)

God repeatedly tells you that you should not be afraid because He is with you. *Why* would you ever be afraid of anything if you are absolutely certain that Almighty God is with you throughout every minute of every hour of every day of your life?

Your Father can do great things in you, through you and for you that you cannot possibly comprehend with the limitations of your human understanding. If you are absolutely certain that God will strengthen you and that He will help you, you will never allow demonic spirits of fear to obtain a foothold in your mind and your heart. You will be calm, quiet and confident deep down inside of yourself. "...in quietness and in confidence shall be your strength..." (Isaiah 30:15 KJV)

If you need the strength of God to help you during a crisis, you must stay close to Him. If you have a close relationship with God, you will receive peace and tranquility from Him regardless of the circumstances you face.

Negative emotions such as fear, worry, anxiety, doubt and unbelief block the strength of God from working in your life. The strength of God will be released in you if you are calm, quiet and confident and refuse to be agitated by whatever problems you face. "...the [Holy] Spirit comes to our aid and bears us up in our weakness..." (Romans 8:26 AMP)

Refuse to identify with your human weakness and inadequacy. Focus continually on the mighty Holy Spirit Who lives in your heart. He will help you when are weak in human ability. "...the joy of the LORD is your strength." (Nehemiah 8:10 KJV)

If you are close to God and trust Him completely, your heart will sing with the joy of the Lord Who is filled with joy. This joy will release His strength in you. God will give you the strength you need one day at a time. "...as your day, so shall your strength, your rest and security, be." (Deuteronomy 33:25 AMP)

Trust God to bring you through today. Stay close to Him throughout this day. Faithfully obey the instructions of Jesus Christ Who said, "...do not worry about tomorrow, for tomorrow will worry about itself. Each day has enough trouble of its own." (Matthew 6:34 NIV)

Jesus does *not* want you to worry about the future. He wants you to live one day at a time. He wants you to stay close to Him throughout each day trusting Him completely to meet every need you have. "This is the day which the LORD hath made; we will rejoice and be glad in it." (Psalm 118:24 KJV)

Rejoice throughout today. Praise God. Thank Him continually. Know that He will bring you safely through today. "Blessed be the Lord, Who bears our burdens and carries us day by day..." (Psalm 68:19 AMP)

Trust God completely to carry the heavy burdens that you cannot carry. Have absolute faith that He will bring you safely through today.

The last two chapters are filled with encouraging truths from the Bible pertaining to the supernatural strength of God that is available to *you*. If you face seemingly insurmountable problems, draw closer to God by meditating day and night on these magnificent promises and any others you find in the Bible. Absolutely refuse to give up because you are certain that you can do *all things* through the strength of Jesus Christ Who lives in your heart.

Chapter 22

Satan Does Not Want You to Be Close to God

You may or may not know very much of what the Bible says about Satan and his demons. The atmosphere around you is filled with God's angels and with Satan's demons. You can be certain that Satan and his demons do not want you to have an intimate relationship with God. They will do everything they can to hinder you from drawing closer to God.

You have seen that God *will* come close to you *if* you come close to Him. Satan always wants the opposite of what God wants. If you make the quality decision to draw closer to God each day, you can expect Satan and his demons to do everything they can to deceive you in any way they can so that you will not accomplish this goal. Satan and his demons know that this intimate relationship and the deep trust that will develop as a result will enable you to walk in victory over them.

If you make the decision to spend quality quiet time with God each day, you probably will find that many distractions will occur. The telephone will ring during your quiet time. People will want to see you about seemingly urgent matters. You may find that family members and friends are concerned because they cannot comprehend the importance of you setting aside quiet time to get away from everyone and everything to draw closer to God each day.

You may or may not understand that Satan and his demons actually can put thoughts into your mind. Have you ever wondered why a beloved disciple betrayed Jesus? This disciple betrayed Jesus because Satan was successful in putting thoughts of betrayal into his mind and then into his heart. "…Satan having already put the thought of betraying Jesus in the heart of Judas Iscariot, Simon's son" (John 13:2 AMP)

There is no question that Satan was able to put thoughts into the mind and ultimately the heart of Judas. Satan and his demons have not gone anywhere. They do not die like human beings do. They are still here.

Satan and his demons are thieves. They will do everything they can to *steal* the awesome opportunity that Jesus has given to you to draw closer to God. Jesus said, "The thief cometh not, but for to steal, and to kill, and to destroy…" (John 10:10 KJV)

Satan and his demons want to steal from you. They want to kill you if they possibly can. They want to destroy you. They will use all of their deceptive skills to try to accomplish these goals.

Satan was able to get into Eve's mind in the Garden of Eden to impose his thoughts on her (see Genesis 3:1-6). The apostle Paul told the Corinthians that he feared that Satan would get into their minds to deter them from total commitment to Jesus Christ. Paul said, "…I am fearful, lest that even as the serpent beguiled Eve by his cunning, so your minds may be corrupted and seduced from wholehearted and sincere and pure devotion to Christ." (II Corinthians 11:3 AMP)

These words that Paul spoke to the Corinthians apply to you today. Satan and his demons are very clever. They have had thousands of years of experience at deceiving people. Satan and his demons have no spiritual authority and power. They rely entirely on deception.

You must not allow Satan and his demons to influence you so that you will not continually draw closer to God. Jesus said, "Behold, I give unto you power to tread on serpents and scorpions, and over all the power of the enemy: and nothing shall by any means hurt you." (Luke 10:19 KJV)

The words "serpents and scorpions" in this verse refer to Satan and his demons. Jesus has given you the power to walk on Satan and his demons. Jesus has put Satan and his demons under your feet in the spiritual realm.

You must understand that you have been given total, complete and absolute authority over Satan and his demons because of the magnificent victory that Jesus Christ won at Calvary (see I John 3:8). Refuse to allow Satan and his demons to deceive you. Deception is their only hope.

Satan's demons will try to get at you through lack of knowledge. If you do not know what the Word of God says about drawing closer to God and what the Bible says about walking in victory over Satan, Satan and his demons will be able to deceive you (see Hosea 4:6). They cannot deceive you if your heart is filled with the Word of God. "...the word of God abideth in you, and ye have overcome the wicked one." (I John 2:14 KJV)

You can and will walk in victory over Satan if you faithfully obey your Father's instructions to meditate day and night on His Word (see James 4:7). When you meditate on God's Word, you fill your heart with the supernatural power of the holy Scriptures.

Another area that is important in drawing closer to God is to do your very best to learn what the Bible teaches about your Father's incredible love for you. God said, "Can a mother forget the baby at her breast and have no compassion on the child she has borne? Though she may forget, I will not forget you!" (Isaiah 49:15 NIV)

What loving mother could forget nurturing her infant children? Your Father says that this unlikely occurrence is much more likely to occur than for Him to forget you.

Your Father loves you. He will not forget you. You should focus on what the Bible says about God's love as you continually draw closer to Him. Jesus said, "If ye keep my commandments, ye shall abide in my love; even as I have kept my Father's commandments, and abide in his love. These things have I spoken unto you, that my joy might remain in you, and that your joy might be full." (John 15:10-11 KJV)

When you abide in the love of Jesus, you *remain* in His love. Every aspect of your life is solidly anchored upon your certainty of His unconditional love for you. You abide in the Word of God by consistently learning what the Bible instructs you to do and then obeying these instructions. You will abide in the love of Jesus Christ if you obey God's instructions just as Jesus remained in His Father's love throughout His earthly ministry because He faithfully obeyed His Father's instructions.

There is a direct relationship between drawing closer to God, experiencing the joy of God and consistently learning and obeying God's specific instructions. The more you know about your Father's love for you, the more likely you will be to continually draw closer to Him. Your life should be deeply rooted in your awareness of God's love for you (see our Scripture Meditation Cards titled *Our Father's Wonderful Love*.)

No matter how difficult the problems you face may seem, you must understand that your Father's love is much greater and much more powerful than any problem you will ever face. "Though the mountains be shaken and the hills be removed, yet my unfailing love for you will not be shaken nor my covenant of peace be removed,' says the LORD, who has compassion on you." (Isaiah 54:10 NIV)

This verse of Scripture says that, even if mountains shake and hills disappear, God's love for you will not waver. Your loving Father can and will bring you safely through every problem you will ever face if you stay close to Him and focus consistently on what His Word says about His great love for you. Bask in God's love. Immerse yourself in God's love. Live in God's love.

Some Christians do not know much about God's love for them. Some people were taught as children that God is a stern taskmaster. They think of God primarily as someone who will punish them.

Try to visualize the most loving father or mother who has ever lived. Try to visualize the love that this parent has for his or her children. Know that God's love for you is infinitely greater than the love that *any* human father or mother has ever had for his or her child. If you spend a considerable amount of time each day drawing closer to God, you will be blessed by the One Who loves you most of all.

When you know God, you love Him. The more intimately you know God, the more you will love Him and the more you will be able to comprehend His great love for you.

Your life should focus around your certainty that God is your loving Father and that you are His beloved child. Do not look at God only as a stern judge. Look at God as your Father Whose great love for you is beyond the limitations of your human comprehension. You can be certain that He "…comforts (consoles and encourages) us in every trouble (calamity and affliction)…" (II Corinthians 1:4 AMP)

No matter what problems you may face at this time, you must understand that your loving Father is right there with you to comfort you and to encourage you. Constantly draw closer to God. Receive by faith and the knowledge of God's Word the great comfort and encouragement that your Father will give you because He loves you so much.

Little children often turn to their mother when they face a problem. These children are secure in their mother's love. Your Father wants you to be certain that He will comfort you just as loving mothers comfort their children. He said, "As one whom his mother comforteth, so will I comfort you…" (Isaiah 66:13 KJV)

No matter what problem you face, you can depend on God. The Bible speaks of "…God, Who comforts and encourages and refreshes and cheers the depressed and the sinking…" (II Corinthians 7:6 AMP)

Are you tempted to give in to depression? Do you feel like you are sinking? Stay so close to God that you will receive His comfort. Instead of giving in to discouragement, receive encouragement from God.

This chapter is filled with facts about Satan and his goal of trying to stop you from drawing closer to God. This chapter contains many truths from the Bible pertaining to your Father's incredible love for you. Constantly draw closer to your Father. Center your life around your absolute certainty that He loves you with a love that is much greater than you can possibly comprehend.

Chapter 23

Trust God to Meet All of Your Needs

You have read about the relationship between living in God's love and enjoying a close relationship with God. There also is a relationship between living in the peace of God and being close to God. Jesus said, "Peace I leave with you; My [own] peace I now give and bequeath to you. Not as the world gives do I give to you. Do not let your hearts be troubled, neither let them be afraid. [Stop allowing yourselves to be agitated and disturbed; and do not permit yourselves to be fearful and intimidated and cowardly and unsettled.]" (John 14:27 AMP)

Jesus spoke these words to His disciples during the last meal He shared with them before His crucifixion. Jesus knew that He soon would be crucified. He wanted His disciples to live in His peace during this ordeal and the turbulent period immediately after He died.

These words also apply to your life today. Jesus has given you His own peace. If you stay close to Him, you will not allow any problems you face to steal the supernatural peace that Jesus has given to you.

Please note the key words "let," "allowing" and "permit" in this verse of Scripture and the amplification. You decide throughout each day of your life whether you will *allow* the peace of Jesus Christ to be taken from you. If you continually stay close to Jesus, you will not give up His supernatural peace. The following anointed words written by the apostle Peter will apply to you. "May grace (God's favor) and peace (which is perfect well-being, all necessary good, all spiritual prosperity, and freedom from fears and agitating passions and moral conflicts) be multiplied to you in [the full, personal, precise, and correct] knowledge of God and of Jesus our Lord." (II Peter 1:2 AMP)

This verse of Scripture explains the relationship between living in God's peace and knowing God intimately. You should have a sense of absolute peace, regardless of the circumstances you face. If you know God intimately, you will be certain that everything is under control regardless of what the external circumstances may look like. God said, "If only you had paid attention to my commands, your peace would have been like a river..." (Isaiah 48:18 NIV)

These words that God spoke to the Israelites many years ago apply to you today. If you stay close to God and consistently live in obedience to His instructions, His supernatural peace will flow through you like a river. You will not give up the peace of God if you have a constant consciousness of His indwelling presence and if every aspect of your life revolves around Him. "...I the LORD thy God will hold thy right hand, saying unto thee, Fear not; I will help thee." (Isaiah 41:13 KJV)

Little children are secure when they are holding onto the hand of one of their loving parents. Your loving Father holds your hand in the spiritual realm. He does not want you to be afraid. He wants you to be absolutely certain that He will help you. "...He [God] Himself has said, I will not in any way fail you nor give you up nor leave you without support. [I will] not, [I will] not, [I will] not in any degree leave you helpless nor forsake nor let [you] down (relax My hold on you)! [Assuredly not!]" (Hebrews 13:5 AMP)

God always emphasizes through repetition. He uses the words "will not" *four* times in this verse of Scripture and the amplification. God wants you to be certain that He will never fail you and that He will never leave you.

Stay close to God. Trust Him completely. Know that He will never let you down. "...we take comfort and are encouraged and confidently and boldly say, The Lord is my Helper; I will not be seized with alarm [I will not fear or dread or be terrified]..." (Hebrews 13:6 AMP)

If you are certain that God will help you, you will not be alarmed by any problem you face. You will not be afraid. You will trust God completely because of the intimacy of your relationship with Him.

Jesus fully understands everything that you are experiencing. He had to cope with many severe problems during His earthly ministry. "...we do not have a High Priest Who is unable to understand and sympathize and have a shared feeling with our weaknesses and infirmities and liability to the assaults of temptation, but One Who has been tempted in every respect as we are, yet without sinning. Let us then fearlessly and confidently and boldly draw near to the throne of grace (the throne of God's unmerited favor to us sinners), that we may receive mercy [for our failures] and find grace to help in good time for every need [appropriate help and well-timed help, coming just when we need it]." (Hebrews 4:15-16 AMP)

Jesus sympathizes with you. He knows exactly how you feel. He wants you to draw close to God so that you will receive God's mercy and grace in whatever ordeal you face.

Jesus promises that God will help you with *every* need if you will stay so close to Him that you trust Him completely. God's timing is perfect. He knows what you need. He knows exactly when you need His help. Your faith that He will help you should be like the faith of the psalmist who said, "My help cometh from the LORD, which made heaven and earth." (Psalm 121:2 KJV)

If God was able to create heaven and earth, He knows how to solve every problem you will ever face. Refuse to give up. Draw closer to God. Meditate continually on these promises that tell you that God *will* help you.

Your loving Father wants you to be absolutely certain that He will provide everything you need. "If anyone fails to provide for his relatives, and especially for those of his own family, he has disowned the faith [by failing to accompany it with fruits] and is worse than an unbeliever [who performs his obligation in these matters]." (I Timothy 5:8 AMP)

This verse of Scripture tells you what God thinks about parents on earth who do not provide for their families. If God feels this strongly about parents who do not take care of their families, how much more importancc do you think He places on His responsibility to provide for the needs of every one of His children? Stay close to your loving Father at all times. Trust Him completely to meet every need that you have. "He that spared not his own Son, but delivered him up for us all, how shall he not with him also freely give us all things?" (Romans 8:32 KJV)

God gave His only Son so that you can live eternally with Him in heaven. If you have trusted God to meet the most important need you will ever have, you also can trust Him completely to meet every other need you will have throughout your life on earth.

The words "all things" in this verse of Scripture include *every* need that you have at this time and every need that you will have in the future.. Stay close to God. Persevere in your faith in Him. "...His divine power has bestowed upon us all things that [are requisite and suited] to life and godliness, through the [full, personal] knowledge of Him Who called us by and to His own glory and excellence (virtue)." (II Peter 1:3 AMP)

Your Father will meet every one of your needs in direct proportion to the intimacy of your relationship with Him and your trust and confidence in Him. "...they who seek (inquire of and require) the Lord [by right of their need and on the authority of His Word], none of them shall lack any beneficial thing." (Psalm 34:10 AMP)

You can trust completely in the authority and power of God's Word. Your Father wants you to know exactly what He has promised to do. "...no good thing will he withhold from them that walk uprightly." (Psalm 84:11 KJV)

The words "no good thing" in this verse of Scripture include whatever you need now and whatever you will need in the future. The words "walk uprightly" mean that you should do your very best to consistently live in obedience to your Father's instructions. "...my God shall supply all your need according to his riches in glory by Christ Jesus." (Philippians 4:19 KJV)

The word "all" in this verse of Scripture definitely includes whatever need you have at this time. There is no question that your Father has promised to meet every need that you have *if* you stay close to Him and persevere with absolute faith in Him.

If you have needs, meditate repeatedly on the promises in this chapter that assure you that your Father *will* supply every one of your needs if you stay close to Him, trust Him completely and faithfully obey the instructions He has given to you. Refuse to give up. Know that your Father always does exactly what He says He will do.

In this chapter you have learned many glorious truths from the Bible about the relationship between your intimacy with God and remaining in His peace at all times. You have learned that your Father will help you. You have learned that your Father promises to provide for every need you will ever have.

God has done His part. You must do your part. Your part is to continually draw closer to Him by living in obedience to the instructions in His Word and by having absolute faith in Him at all times.

Chapter 24

Effective Prayer

In this chapter we will look into the Bible for information about the relationship between effective prayer and an intimate relationship with God. If you are close to God, you will immediately pray whenever you face adversity. "Is any one of you in trouble? He should pray…" (James 5:13 NIV)

If you love God, you will talk with Him every day. Whenever you face a problem, you will talk with Him even more. Your Father wants to help you. If you have a close relationship with Him, you will be certain that He will help you. "…the prayer of the upright is his delight." (Proverbs 15:8 KJV)

Your Father is delighted when you come to Him in prayer. He is pleased when you turn to Him with absolute faith in Him instead of thinking that you have to find the solution to your problems from worldly sources. "We know that God does not listen to sinners; but if anyone is God-fearing and a worshiper of Him and does His will, He listens to him." (John 9:31 AMP)

God does not listen to the prayers of people who have never received His Son as their Savior. He does listen to the prayers of each of His children who revere Him and adore Him. If you have a close relationship with God and your life revolves around your certainty of His indwelling presence, you can be certain that your Father listens to you when you pray. "And this is the confidence (the assurance, the privilege of boldness) which we have in Him: [we are sure] that if we ask anything (make any request) according to His will (in agreement with His own plan), He listens to and hears us." (I John 5:14 AMP)

God's general will for all of His children is explained in the Bible. If your prayers are based on God's Word, you can be certain that you are praying according to your Father's will for your life. "And if (since) we [positively] know that He listens to us in whatever we ask, we also know [with settled and absolute knowledge] that we have [granted us as our present possessions] the requests made of Him." (I John 5:15 AMP)

Please notice that the word "know" is used two times in this verse of Scripture. If you are close to God, you will know that your loving Father hears each of your prayers. You will know that your prayers will be answered.

The words "present possessions" in the amplification of this verse of Scripture are very important. If you pray according to God's will, He answers your prayers *when you pray*. God answers immediately in the spiritual realm.

You may not receive manifestation of God's answer immediately in the natural realm. If you do not receive His answer as soon as you think you should, know that your prayer already has been answered in the spiritual realm. Keep thanking God for answering your prayer.

Your Father wants you to stay close to Him and to trust Him completely. Persevere with deep, strong and unwavering faith in God for as long as He requires you to persevere.

If you have an intimate relationship with Jesus and your heart is filled with His Word, you will be absolutely certain that He answers your prayers. Jesus said, "If you live in Me [abide vitally united to Me] and My words remain in you and continue to live in your hearts, ask whatever you will, and it shall be done for you." (John 15:7 AMP)

Jesus explains two conditions that must be present for you to be certain that He will answer your prayers. The words "abide vitally united to Me" in the amplification of this verse of Scripture are very important. A close relationship with Jesus is not an option. A close relationship with Jesus is vitally important.

In addition to being very close to Jesus with every aspect of your life revolving around your certainty of His indwelling presence, the other condition is for your heart to be filled with His Word. You have learned that the Word of God goes into your *mind* when you *study* the Bible and then drops down into your *heart* when you consistently *meditate* day and night on the Word of God.

If you have meditated day and night on God's Word for many months or years, your heart will be filled with God's Word. You will have absolute confidence that God answers your prayers. Jesus said, "...I tell you the truth, my Father will give you whatever you ask in my name." (John 16:23 NIV)

The name of Jesus Christ has supernatural power. You should have absolute faith in the mighty power of the name of Jesus (see I John 3:23). If you are continually conscious of the indwelling presence of Jesus Christ and you have an intimate relationship with Him, you will pray to God in the name of Jesus.

When you come to your Father with a prayer of faith in the name of His beloved Son, your prayer has the same significance as if Jesus Himself was praying to God. Know that God answers your prayers when you come to Him in the name of Jesus with absolute faith. Jesus said, "...whatever you ask for in prayer, believe (trust and be confident) that it is granted to you, and you will [get it]." (Mark 11:24 AMP)

God's promises to answer prayers are conditional. You must pray, but you also must have absolute faith that God will answer your prayers. "...whatsoever we ask, we receive of him, because we keep his commandments, and do those things that are pleasing in his sight." (I John 3:22 KJV)

You have just read three verses of Scripture where you are told that you *will* receive whatever you ask of God in prayer. This verse explains the relationship between God answering all of your prayers and your faithful obedience to the instructions He has given you in His Book of Instructions, the Bible.

You cannot know what your Father has instructed you to do if you do not study His Word each day and meditate day and night on the holy Scriptures. If your prayers are solidly anchored upon faith in

God and His Word, they will be effective. "...The earnest (heartfelt, continued) prayer of a righteous man makes tremendous power available [dynamic in its working]." (James 5:16 AMP)

When you pray earnestly, you are serious, sincere and determined. Your prayers are vigorous, concentrated and focused. If you are close to God and you trust Him completely, your prayers will be earnest prayers.

These prayers of faith from your heart will release the supernatural power of God. If you believe this great spiritual truth, your prayers will be effective. You will not pray the way that many religious people pray. Jesus said, "...when you pray, do not heap up phrases (multiply words, repeating the same ones over and over) as the Gentiles do, for they think they will be heard for their much speaking." (Matthew 6:7 AMP)

Your Father does not require you to pray formally using the language in the *King James Version* of the Bible. He does not want you to pray the same words day after day. Just speak your heart. Your Father wants you to have such a close relationship with Him that your prayers will be spontaneous, natural and filled with faith.

When you know someone intimately, you talk with this person often. This same principle applies to praying to God. You should be so close to your Father that you pray using a similar vocabulary to the words that you use when you talk with people who are close to you.

Your Father wants you to talk with Him as the close and intimate Friend that He is. He wants you to hold Him in reverence and awe, but He does not want you to be stiff and formal when you pray.

If you have a close relationship with God, you will pray to Him throughout each day and night of your life. "Be unceasing in prayer [praying perseveringly]" (I Thessalonians 5:17 AMP)

In addition to praying to God many times each day, you also should have a place where you go for specific daily prayer time. Jesus said, "...when you pray, go into your [most] private room, and, closing the door, pray to your Father, Who is in secret; and your Father, Who sees in secret, will reward you in the open." (Matthew 6:6 AMP)

Jesus instructs you to go to a specific place for prayer each day. In addition to this regular daily prayer time, you should pray on many other occasions. Your Father wants to hear you praying continually. We recommend that you pray whenever you hear a siren. The sound of a siren is a clear indication that someone is in trouble. Pray for that person. When you read an article in a newspaper or hear about someone who faces adversity, pray for that person. "Pray at all times (on every occasion, in every season) in the Spirit, with all [manner of] prayer and entreaty. To that end keep alert and watch with strong purpose and perseverance, interceding in behalf of all the saints (God's consecrated people)." (Ephesians 6:18 AMP)

You should always be alert for the opportunity to pray for people, particularly other Christians. Ask the Holy Spirit to guide you. "...You do not have, because you do not ask God. When you ask, you do not receive, because you ask with wrong motives, that you may spend what you get on your pleasures." (James 4:2-3 NIV)

Some people do not receive answers from God because they do not go to Him in prayer. Your motivation is very important when you pray. You often will block God from answering if all or most of your prayers are selfish and greedy.

This chapter is filled with truth from the Bible about praying effectively. If you are close to God, you *will* pray continually. Your Father *will* answer your prayers. Now that we have studied what God's Word says about effective prayer, we are ready to learn what the Bible says about continually thanking God and praising Him.

Chapter 25

Praise God Continually

If you have an intimate relationship with God and you trust Him completely, you will thank Him when you face adversity. *Why* should you thank God in the face of adversity? You should thank Him because you know that Jesus has given you victory over every problem you face. "...thanks be to God, which giveth us the victory through our Lord Jesus Christ." (I Corinthians 15:57 KJV)

If Jesus Christ is your Savior, you can be certain that He lives in your heart (see II Corinthians 13:5, Galatians 2:20, Ephesians 3:17 and I John 3:24). Instead of focusing on whatever problem you face, you should focus continually on the victorious Jesus Christ Who lives in your heart. You should be so close to Him that you will always thank God. "Offer to God the sacrifice of thanksgiving, and pay your vows to the Most High" (Psalm 50:14 AMP)

When you thank God in the face of seemingly severe adversity, you are making a *sacrifice*. You are stepping out in faith because you are so close to your Father that you trust Him completely. You are thanking God in the face of adversity even though thanking Him does not make any sense from a logical, worldly and intellectual perspective.

When you offer a sacrifice of praise and thanksgiving to God, you may find yourself crying. These are healthy, healing tears. When you speak with God, your emotions come alive. Your tears of sadness actually become tears of joy because of the presence of God.

If you have a constant attitude of gratitude to God and you live your life in His presence, you *will* thank Him at all times regardless of the circumstances you face. "He who brings an offering of praise and thanksgiving honors and glorifies Me..." (Psalm 50:23 AMP)

When you praise God and thank Him regardless of the circumstances you face, you are making an offering to God that is just as significant as any financial offering you put into a collection plate at a church. You give God what is due Him when you consistently give Him an offering of praise and thanksgiving. "This people have I formed for myself; they shall shew forth my praise." (Isaiah 43:21 KJV)

If you knew that God created you for a specific purpose, wouldn't you place great importance on doing what God created you to do? You must understand that God created you to praise Him. "Great is the LORD and most worthy of praise; his greatness no one can fathom." (Psalm 145:3 NIV)

God is so awesome that praise should continually well up from deep within your heart. God is much greater and much more powerful than you can possibly comprehend. He loves you so much that He sacrificed His only Son so that you can live eternally with Him in heaven.

If you can even begin to comprehend the enormity of the price that Jesus paid for you on the cross at Calvary, deep gratitude will fill your heart. You cannot praise God and thank Him enough. Praising God should be a way of life to you. "From the rising of the sun to the going down of it and from east to west, the name of the Lord is to be praised!" (Psalm 113:3 AMP)

Do not limit your praise. The Bible instructs you to praise God from morning until night wherever you are. If you truly have a close relationship with God, you will praise Him continually.

You should be so close to God and trust Him so much that you will be consistent in your praise regardless of the circumstances you face. Praise was a way of life to the psalmist David. He said, "The Lord is my Strength and my [impenetrable] Shield; my heart trusts in, relies on, and confidently leans on Him, and I am helped; therefore my heart greatly rejoices, and with my song will I praise Him." (Psalm 28:7 AMP)

You should praise God when you are on the mountaintops of life. You should praise Him when you are deep in valleys. David said, "I will bless the Lord at all times; His praise shall continually be in my mouth." (Psalm 34:1 AMP)

If you truly are close to God, you will be certain that He will provide the strength you need and that He will protect you at all times (see Psalm 29:11, Proverbs 29:25, Isaiah 40:28-31 and Philippians 4:13). You will be certain that He will help you. Because you trust Him completely, your heart will sing with joy. You will be like the psalmist who said, "My mouth is filled with your praise, declaring your splendor all day long." (Psalm 71:8 NIV)

If your heart is filled with gratitude to God, this gratitude will pour out of your lips. You will praise God continually. The more you praise God in the face of seemingly severe adversity, the closer you will draw to Him. "...let us offer the sacrifice of praise to God continually, that is, the fruit of our lips giving thanks to his name." (Hebrews 13:15 KJV)

Once again you are told to make a *sacrifice* when you praise God. You make a sacrifice when you are so close to God and trust Him so much that you praise Him and thank Him when there does not seem to be any worldly reason to praise Him and thank Him. When you do this, you will experience "...beauty instead of ashes, the oil of joy instead of mourning, the garment [expressive] of praise instead of a heavy, burdened, and failing spirit" (Isaiah 61:3 AMP)

When you are tempted to be discouraged by the problems you face, Satan's demons will attempt to get into your mind to influence you to be depressed. Refuse to give a foothold to Satan and his demons. Praise God continually.

The Bible compares praise to a garment. A garment is a piece of clothing that covers part of your body. You are instructed to cover yourself spiritually with praise at all times just as you cover your body with clothing.

If you obey these instructions, God will give you His beauty and His joy. You will not receive the spiritual "ashes" that Satan's demons will attempt to put on you. "Let the people praise thee, O God; let all the people praise thee. Then shall the earth yield her increase; and God, even our own God, shall bless us." (Psalm 67:5-6 KJV)

God instructs *everyone* to praise Him, regardless of the circumstances they face. If you praise God continually, He will bless you. God will cause the earth to give you an increase. "As the refining pot for silver and the furnace for gold [bring forth all the impurities of the metal], so let a man be in his trial of praise [ridding himself of all that is base or insincere; for a man is judged by what he praises and of what he boasts]." (Proverbs 27:21 AMP)

When this verse of Scripture was written, silver was put into a refining pot and gold was put into a furnace to remove impurities. If you trust God so much that you praise Him at all times, He will cause the adversity you face to work in such a way so as to remove impurities from you.

The word "base" in the amplification of this verse means to be ungrateful and negative. God will take any tendency to be negative away from you if you praise Him consistently. Your emotions will be cleansed.

The apostle Paul and a man named Silas were put into a damp and dark Roman prison because they told other people about their faith in Jesus Christ. How did Paul and Silas react to this imprisonment? They did not feel sorry for themselves. "...at midnight Paul and Silas prayed, and sang praises unto God: and the prisoners heard them. And suddenly there was a great earthquake, so that the foundations of the prison were shaken: and immediately all the doors were opened, and every one's bands were loosed." (Acts 16:25-26 KJV)

Paul and Silas prayed and sang praise to God. God suddenly performed a mighty miracle. A powerful earthquake unfastened the chains that bound them. They were set free.

This same principle applies to you today. You should be so close to God and trust Him so much that you will praise Him continually, regardless of the circumstances you face. Paul and Silas were so close to Jesus that they refused to feel sorry for themselves because they were in prison. They praised God instead of complaining.

We believe that continual praise, worship and thanksgiving releases the power of mighty angels to come into action on your behalf. We believe that a continual attitude of praise, worship and thanksgiving dispels Satan and his demons from any opportunity to influence you with the negative and destructive thoughts they want to put into your mind.

God's ways are much higher and very different from the ways of the world. If you are so close to God that you trust Him totally, completely and absolutely regardless of the circumstances you face, you will praise Him and thank Him just as the Scripture we have been studying instructs you to do.

Now that we have studied basic instructions from God on the topics of praise, worship and thanksgiving, we are ready to look more deeply into God's Word. You will see that a constant attitude of thanksgiving and praise *actually will bring you into the presence of God.*

Chapter 26

Sing Praise to God

The Bible contains many instructions pertaining to praising God. We now will study the relationship between being close to God and *singing* your praise to Him. In this chapter we will study several verses of Scripture that specifically instruct you to sing praise to God. "Sing praises to God, sing praises; sing praises to our King, sing praises. For God is the King of all the earth; sing to him a psalm of praise." (Psalm 47:6-7 NIV)

God emphasizes through repetition. When your Father instructs you *five times* in one short passage of Scripture to sing praises to Him, you can be certain that singing praises to God is very important.

You should have such an intimate relationship with God and your heart should be so filled with gratitude toward Him that songs of praise will spontaneously pour out of your mouth throughout each day and night of your life. "Praise the Lord! For it is good to sing praises to our God, for He is gracious and lovely; praise is becoming and appropriate." (Psalm 147:1 AMP)

Your loving Father has given you many blessings that you did not earn and do not deserve. The more you learn about God's awesome grace, mercy, love and compassion for you, the more desire you will have to praise Him.

If your heart sings with joy because of Who your Father is and everything He has done for you, the joy in your heart will constantly be expressed by songs of praise to God. "…Is anyone glad at heart? He should sing praise [to God]." (James 5:13 AMP)

Are you deeply grateful to God? Are you filled with gratitude to Jesus for what He did for *you* when He gave His life for *you* on the cross at Calvary? If you have this deep gratitude, your heart will be filled with joy. The joy that fills your heart will be expressed by singing songs of praise to God. "My heart is fixed, O God, my heart is fixed: I will sing and give praise." (Psalm 57:7 KJV)

Once again God emphasizes through repetition. He used the words "my heart is fixed" consecutively in this verse of Scripture. When more than fifty percent of one short verse of Scripture consists of the same words repeated twice, you can be certain that your Father is emphasizing the importance of a heart that is fixed.

A fixed heart is a heart that is filled with the Word of God. Christians whose hearts are filled to overflowing with the holy Scriptures always have a close and intimate relationship with God. They will praise God continually regardless of the circumstances they face. You should be like the psalmist who said, "I will praise you, O LORD, with all my heart; I will tell of all your wonders. I will be glad and rejoice in you; I will sing praise to your name, O Most High." (Psalm 9:1-2 NIV)

If your loving Father has helped you to come safely through adversity in the past, you can trust Him to do the same when you face adversity now and in the future. You should praise Him and thank Him for His past blessings and because you are certain that He will help you again. As you boldly express your faith in God, the joy in your heart will pour out of your mouth as you sing praise to God. "Then [Israel] believed His words [trusting in, relying on them]; they sang His praise." (Psalm 106:12 AMP)

This verse of Scripture compares singing praise with the trust the Israelites had in God when He led them through the Red Sea. If your heart is filled with God's Word and you have a close relationship with God, songs of praise will flow out of your mouth. "Make a joyful noise unto the LORD, all the earth: make a loud noise, and rejoice, and sing praise." (Psalm 98:4 KJV)

Your Father wants every person on earth to open his or her mouth to loudly sing praise to Him. We are so excited to see some of our children and grandchildren developing their musical abilities. God provided music for us to enable us to express our deepest emotions and our love and gratitude to Him.

You should not be inhibited. When you praise God, you should sing constantly, praising Him with all your heart. The more fervently you praise God, the closer you will be to Him and the more conscious you will be of His magnificent indwelling presence. "...let all those who take refuge and put their trust in You rejoice; let them ever sing and shout for joy, because You make a covering over them and defend them; let those also who love Your name be joyful in You and be in high spirits." (Psalm 5:11 AMP)

Your loving Father wants you to take refuge in Him and to put all of your trust in Him. He wants you to constantly sing and shout for joy because you are absolutely certain that He is protecting you. "It is a good and delightful thing to give thanks to the Lord, to sing praises [with musical accompaniment] to Your name, O Most High" (Psalm 92:1 AMP)

The amplification of this verse of Scripture uses the words "with musical accompaniment." We have found that playing recorded worship music helps us to sing praises to God. We frequently play recorded worship music in our home and in our cars. We sing along with this music.

We have found that repeatedly singing praise to God programs us so that a subconscious undercurrent of praise flows through us at all times. This subliminal praise is magnificent. Singing praise to God will energize you and refresh you.

An excellent source of praise and worship music is Gaither music at www.gaither.com (1-800-955-8746). We have more than one hundred Gaither music videos and DVDs in our home. We also have many of their CDs and cassette tapes.

We do not know of any Christian organization that has done a more effective job of providing magnificent praise and worship music than Bill and Gloria Gaither and their associates. We recommend them highly because we know from experience that consistently listening to and singing along with their anointed praise and worship music will draw you closer to God.

God spoke to King Jehoshaphat when the Israelites faced overwhelming opposition from armies consisting of warriors from Moab and Ammon. God instructed King Jehoshaphat and his followers not to be afraid of this mighty army because He would fight the battle for them. God said, "You shall not need to fight in this battle; take your positions, stand still, and see the deliverance of the Lord [Who is] with you, O Judah and Jerusalem. Fear not nor be dismayed. Tomorrow go out against them, for the Lord is with you." (II Chronicles 20:17 AMP)

These words that God spoke to the Israelites many years ago apply to you today. If you have a close relationship with God, you will not be worried, afraid or agitated. You will be quiet, calm and confident in God. "And Jehoshaphat bowed his head with his face to the ground, and all Judah and the inhabitants of Jerusalem fell down before the Lord, worshiping Him." (II Chronicles 20:18 AMP)

King Jehoshaphat did what your Father wants you to do when you face severe adversity. God wants you to worship Him just as the Israelites did when they "…stood up to praise the Lord, the God of Israel, with a very loud voice." (II Chronicles 20:19 AMP)

Do you face severe problems? If you trust God completely, you will praise Him. Your Father does not want you to be timid when you praise Him. He wants you to praise Him boldly. "When he had consulted with the people, he appointed singers to sing to the Lord and praise Him in their holy [priestly] garments as they went out before the army, saying, Give thanks to the Lord, for His mercy and lovingkindness endure forever!" (II Chronicles 20:21 AMP)

When King Jehoshaphat faced seemingly overwhelming opposition, he appointed singers to sing to God and praise Him. You should follow this example in your life. When you face seemingly severe problems, you should constantly *sing* praises to God and thank Him because you have total, complete and absolute faith in Him.

If you consistently praise God and sing to Him, He will respond to your joyful heart just as He did for King Jehoshaphat and the Israelites. "…when they began to sing and to praise, the Lord set ambushments against the men of Ammon, Moab, and Mount Seir who had come against Judah, and they were [self-] slaughtered"(II Chronicles 20:22 AMP)

Please stop for a moment to meditate on this verse of Scripture. Think about how God responded to the Israelites when they sang praises to Him in the face of seemingly overwhelming opposition. He overcame their enemies.

Believe that God will respond favorably when you repeatedly indicate your faith in Him by singing praises to Him. "...ever be filled and stimulated with the [Holy] Spirit. Speak out to one another in psalms and hymns and spiritual songs, offering praise with voices [and instruments] and making melody with all your heart to the Lord, at all times and for everything giving thanks in the name of our Lord Jesus Christ to God the Father." (Ephesians 5:18-20 AMP)

You will be filled with the Spirit if you consistently sing praise to God because your heart is filled with gratitude toward God. If you sing praise to God along with musical instruments from anointed Christian musicians, we believe you will find that this praise will draw you closer to the Holy Spirit Who lives in your heart.

Your Father wants you to spend a significant amount of time each day singing praise to Him as you pour out your adoration to Him. If you do, you will become quiet, calm and confident deep down inside of yourself.

If you are tired and weary and you are tempted to be discouraged, play some anointed praise and worship music on an MP3 player, an Ipod, a CD player, a cassette player, a DVD or a videotape. Boldly sing along with this anointed music. As you continue to sing praise and worship to God, you will be energized and strengthened. "...You are holy, O You Who dwell in [the holy place where] the praises of Israel [are offered]." (Psalm 22:3 AMP)

When the Israelites praised God, their praise brought them into the holy place where God was. This same spiritual phenomenon applies to you today. Continual praise will bring you into God's presence. The Bible says that you come into God's presence when you thank Him continually. "Let us come before his presence with thanksgiving..." (Psalm 95:2 KJV)

If your heart is filled with gratitude to God, you will express this joy by singing praise and worship to Him. As you consistently express your gratitude to God in song, you will come more and more into His presence. "Make a joyful noise unto the LORD, all ye lands. Serve the Lord with gladness: come before his presence with singing." (Psalm 100:1-2 KJV)

The words "come before his presence with singing" in this passage of Scripture are extremely important. If you consistently sing praise to God, you *will* come into His glorious presence. "Enter into His gates with thanksgiving and a thank offering and into His courts with praise! Be thankful and say so to Him, bless and affectionately praise His name!" (Psalm 100:4 AMP)

You will draw closer to God when you thank Him continually. When you consistently praise Him, you will come directly into His presence. There is no safer place in the entire universe than to be in the presence of God (see Psalm 91:9-10). If you are in the presence of God, you will experience the epitome of a close and intimate relationship with Him.

Are you consistently singing praise to God? If your heart is filled with God's Word and if you have an intimate relationship with God, nothing will be more normal and natural to you than to praise God spontaneously.

In this chapter we have given you an introduction to coming into the presence of God. In the next chapter we will study additional verses of Scripture so that you can learn more about what God teaches about how to come into His presence and remain there.

Chapter 27

The Privilege of Coming into the Presence of God

We believe that the last two chapters are two of the most important, if not the most important, chapters in this book. These chapters explain what your Father instructs you to do to come into His presence. *What could be more important* to a close and intimate relationship with God than to know exactly what He instructs you to do to come into His presence? Because of the importance of the spiritual truths contained in the last two chapters, we will begin this chapter by summarizing and reviewing the contents of these two chapters.

Psalm 100:4 explains that you enter into God's gates when you *thank* Him and that you enter into His courts when you *praise* Him. Consistent thanksgiving opens spiritual doors for you to come into the presence of God. Consistent praise will bring you into the presence of God.

You should thank God for everything He does. You should praise God because of Who He is. Some Scripture indicates that you also should praise God for what He has done. You should have a constant attitude of gratitude. *If* your heart is filled with gratitude to God, you *will* constantly praise Him and thank Him. Words of praise and thanksgiving will pour out of your mouth many times each day.

If you have a deep attitude of gratitude, praise and thanksgiving will be a normal and natural part of your everyday life. You will consistently come into the presence of God. Coming into the presence of God is not complicated.

If you truly are grateful to God and your heart is filled with gratitude, you will *not* be able to stop yourself from continually thanking God and praising Him. The gratitude that fills your heart will pour out of your mouth (see Matthew 12:34).

Everything that you have and everything that you are is yours because of your Father's love, mercy and grace. You did not earn and you do not deserve any of the blessings you have received.

You should have eternal gratitude to Jesus Christ for the enormous price that He paid when He willingly was crucified to pay the full price for all of your sins. Jesus has provided you with eternal salvation that will enable you to live in the glory of heaven throughout eternity. He also has provided a magnificent victory for you throughout your life on earth. You should have a deep inner desire to thank Jesus and praise Him continually.

We studied Psalm 100:2 where you are told that you come into the presence of God through *singing*. If you truly are grateful to God, your heart will sing with joy. This joy will pour out of your mouth if you consistently sing praise to God.

Have you had the experience of attending church and participating with other Christians in singing glorious songs of praise and worship to God? Have you felt God's presence in this church as you joined with other believers to sing songs of praise and thanksgiving to Him? You do not have to be in church to sing songs of praise and thanksgiving to God. You have the opportunity to come into God's presence throughout every day of your life.

Coming into the presence of God was very complicated before Jesus died at Calvary. Moses built a tabernacle following specific instructions that God gave him. This tabernacle consisted of two rooms. The outer room was called the Holy Place. The inner room was called the Holy of Holies. A thick veil was placed between these two rooms to protect the Holy of Holies.

A selected high priest was able to enter the tabernacle to come into the presence of God on one day each year after the Day of Atonement. Jesus removed the veil between the Holy Place and the Holy of Holies so that *you* can come into the presence of God if Jesus is your Savior. "...we have full freedom and confidence to enter into the [Holy of] Holies [by the power and virtue] in the blood of Jesus, by this fresh (new) and living way which He initiated and dedicated and opened for us through the separating curtain (veil of the Holy of Holies), that is, through His flesh" (Hebrews 10:19-20 AMP)

You are completely free to come into the presence of God at any time because Jesus paid the price for you to come into God's presence. "...Jesus cried with a loud voice, and gave up the ghost. And the veil of the temple was rent in twain from the top to the bottom." (Mark 15:37-38 KJV)

These words apply to the final minute when Jesus gave up His life after suffering for approximately three hours on the cross. Please notice that Jesus was still strong enough after this ordeal to cry out loudly just before He released His human life.

Enormous spiritual power was released when Jesus cried out with a loud voice. This power tore the veil between the Holy Place and the Holy of Holies from the top to the bottom. This phenomenon gave *you* the ability to come into God's presence because of the shed blood of Jesus Christ.

No person is able to enter the presence of God based upon his or her worthiness. You have been made worthy to come into God's presence because the shed blood of Jesus Christ has cleansed you from all sin (see John 1:7).

Coming into God's presence no longer is limited to a high priest coming into God's presence one day each year. If Jesus Christ is your Savior, you do not have to go through a priest, a minister or anyone else to come directly into the presence of God. There is nothing to stop you from coming into God's presence at *any* time.

Many Christians stop themselves from coming into God's presence because they do not know and understand these wonderful truths from the Bible about their ability to come into God's presence. They do not understand what they are instructed to do to come into the presence of God. The apostle Paul explained this truth to the church in Corinth when he said, "...some of you have not the knowledge of

God [you are utterly and willfully and disgracefully ignorant, and continue to be so, lacking the sense of God's presence and all true knowledge of Him]...." (I Corinthians 15:34 AMP)

No unbeliever has a close relationship with God. Unfortunately, many Christians do not have an intimate relationship with God because they do not know what the Bible says in regard to coming into the presence of God.

This book is filled with scriptural truths pertaining to your ability to come into God's presence and to enjoy a close and intimate relationship with God at all times. *Are you* in absolute awe of the fact that *you* have been given the ability to come into the presence of God?

God is unique. No person on earth can remotely compare to Him. You must understand the tremendous blessing that *you* have been given to draw close to God and to come into His presence. God said, "...I am God, and there is no one else; I am God, and there is none like Me" (Isaiah 46:9 AMP)

The opportunity that you have been given to continually come into the presence of God is beyond the limits of human comprehension and understanding. The following verse of Scripture explains the magnitude of being able to come into God's presence. "The earth trembled, the heavens also poured down [rain] at the presence of God; yonder Sinai quaked at the presence of God, the God of Israel." (Psalm 68:8 AMP)

The ability to come into God's presence is so overwhelming that the psalmist explained how the entire earth trembled before the presence of God. Rain poured down from heaven because of the presence of God. An earthquake occurred on Mt. Sinai because of the presence of God.

If God's presence is *this* powerful, you should be in awe of the magnificent privilege you have been given to enter into His presence. You should be highly motivated to learn all of the scriptural truth you can so that you will be able to continually enter into the presence of God. "Tremble, thou earth, at the presence of the Lord, at the presence of the God of Jacob" (Psalm 114:7 KJV)

You should *tremble* because of your understanding that *you* actually have been given the ability to come into the majestic presence of God. We do not have words in our worldly vocabulary that can even begin to explain the magnificence of the privilege of coming into God's presence.

You are only able to enter into God's presence because of your Father's love, grace, compassion and mercy and because of the price that Jesus Christ paid for you. You should be very humble about the privilege you have been given of being able to come into the presence of God. "...no mortal man should [have pretense for glorying and] boast in the presence of God." (I Corinthians 1:29 AMP)

Paul explained to the Corinthians that no human being should boast about anything when he or she is in the presence of God. You should look at yourself as Paul did when he said, "...I know that nothing good dwells within me, that is, in my flesh..." (Romans 7:18 AMP)

Proud people cannot come into the presence of God. The Bible says that God resists people who are proud (see James 4:6 and I Peter 5:5). You cannot possibly enter into God's presence if He is resisting you.

Only humble Christians can come into the presence of God. You will become much more humble when you are in His presence. You will be in absolute awe of God as you observe how magnificent He is and how insignificant you are. "Humble yourselves [feeling very insignificant] in the presence of the Lord, and He will exalt you [He will lift you up and make your lives significant]." (James 4:10 AMP)

If you truly are humble because of the tremendous privilege you have been given of coming into God's presence, He will lift you up and cause your life on earth to be meaningful. If you truly are humble concerning the awesome privilege you have been given of coming into the presence God, He will honor your humility. He will do great things in you, through and for you if you willingly acknowledge how insignificant you are and how great, awesome and magnificent He is.

This chapter is filled with truth from the holy Scriptures pertaining to the wonderful privilege of coming into the presence of God. In the next chapter you will learn additional truths from the Bible about the opportunity that you have been given to come into God's presence and to *remain* there.

Chapter 28

You Can Live Continually
in the Presence of God

Are you highly motivated to live in the presence of God after reading the great scriptural truths in the last chapter? Are you like the psalmist David who said, "One thing have I asked of the Lord, that will I seek, inquire for, and [insistently] require: that I may dwell in the house of the Lord [in His presence] all the days of my life, to behold and gaze upon the beauty [the sweet attractiveness and the delightful loveliness] of the Lord and to meditate, consider, and inquire in His temple."? (Psalm 27:4 AMP)

You should desire to learn everything you can about coming into the presence of God. Your Father wants you to live in His presence throughout every day of your life. He wants you to behold His beauty and splendor. He wants you to understand the awesome privilege that you have been given of being in His presence continually. "...the upright shall dwell in Your presence (before Your very face)." (Psalm 140:13 AMP)

The word "upright" in this verse of Scripture refers to righteousness before God. If Jesus Christ is your Savior, you *are* upright before God. When you dwell in a place, you live there permanently. "Seek the Lord and His strength; yearn for and seek His face and to be in His presence continually!" (I Chronicles 16:11 AMP)

When you yearn for something, you have a deep desire for whatever you yearn for. Your desire to be in God's presence should be the absolute top priority in your life. Every aspect of your life should revolve around the intimacy of your relationship with God.

Most Christians would like to be in the presence of God, but you must do more than to just want an intimate relationship with God. You should have a fervent desire to live in His presence.

You should have deep appreciation for the marvelous opportunity you have been given to come into the presence of God. Do not waste this precious privilege. God does not want you to seek Him occasionally. You are instructed to seek God continually. Would your Father have instructed you to be in His presence *continually* if this were not possible?

The more you come into God's presence, the more you will yearn to remain in His presence. "Blessed (happy, fortunate, to be envied) are those who dwell in Your house and Your presence; they will be singing Your praises all the day long...." (Psalm 84:4 AMP)

Your Father wants you to grow and mature to the degree that you will *remain* in His presence. You will achieve this goal if you consistently sing the praise to God that wells up from your grateful heart.

You have seen specific instructions from the Bible that tell you exactly what to do to come into God's presence. If you consistently study and meditate on these scriptural instructions and promises and if you faithfully obey these instructions and wholeheartedly believe these promises, you *will* come into God's presence. Our Father promises to "...reassure (quiet, conciliate, and pacify) our hearts in His presence." (I John 3:19 AMP)

If you do not have a deep and intimate personal relationship with God and you do not know how to come into His presence, you will be vulnerable to being overwhelmed by seemingly severe problems. If you learn how to come into God's presence and if you obey these instructions, your Father will reassure you. You will experience His wonderful peace. You will be quiet and calm at all times because you are in His presence. "...he said, My presence shall go with thee, and I will give thee rest." (Exodus 33:14 KJV)

You will rest in God when you are in His presence. You will trust Him completely. "Thou wilt shew me the path of life: in thy presence is fulness of joy; at thy right hand there are pleasures for evermore." (Psalm 16:11 KJV)

When you are in God's presence, your Father will show you exactly what He wants you to do with your life. He will guide you every step of the way. When you are in His presence, your heart will overflow with joy. You will experience great pleasure, meaning and fulfillment in your life.

Negative emotions cannot exist in God's presence. You will not be worried, anxious or fearful. You will rejoice regardless of the circumstances you face because of your absolute certainty that your loving Father can and will bring you through every problem you face.

You have just seen that your heart will overflow with joy when you are in God's presence. Your heart should be filled with joy throughout the remainder of your life on earth and throughout eternity in heaven. Everyone in heaven is filled with joy continually because everyone in heaven is continually in the presence of God.

You will be filled with joy here on earth and throughout eternity if you learn now how to come into the presence of God and faithfully obey the instructions your Father has given to you. "You have made known to me the ways of life; You will enrapture me [diffusing my soul with joy] with and in Your presence." (Acts 2:28 AMP)

The word "enrapture" is extremely important. The word "rapture" means to be carried away with joy and ecstasy. The prefix "en" means "in." When you are in God's presence, you will be filled with joy and ecstasy deep down inside of yourself. God's joy will fill your soul to overflowing when you are in His presence.

Your soul consists of your mind, your emotions and your will. Your thoughts will be filled with joy when you are in God's presence. Your emotions will be filled with joy. The decisions that you make will be filled with joy because they will be wise decisions that are guided by God because you are in His presence.

There is no safer place in the world than to be in the presence of God. Most people in the world look for security from external sources. All of the security that you will ever need is provided for you when you are in the presence of God. "He who dwells in the secret place of the Most High shall remain stable and fixed under the shadow of the Almighty [Whose power no foe can withstand]." (Psalm 91:1 AMP)

God's presence is a secret place that is unknown to all unbelievers and, unfortunately, to many believers. The words "Most High" refer to God. You will dwell in the secret place of God's presence if you learn how to come into His presence and stay there.

You will be calm, steady and filled with faith when you are in the presence of God. When this verse refers to the shadow of God, it refers to being so close to God that you actually are under His shadow in the spiritual realm. His supernatural power will protect you at all times.

There is no question that the words "secret place" refer to the presence of God. The psalmist David said, "In the secret place of Your presence You hide them from the plots of men…" (Psalm 31:20 AMP)

Your Father will protect you from being harmed by other people when you are in the secret place of His presence. You will trust God completely when you are in His presence. "I will say of the LORD, He is my refuge and my fortress: my God; in him will I trust." (Psalm 91:2 KJV)

A refuge is a safe place where you are protected. A fortress is a place that has been strengthened to provide additional protection. When you are in God's presence, you will speak of your certainty that God is protecting you.

No matter what is taking place in the world around you, you *will* be protected if you remain in God's presence. "A thousand may fall at your side, and ten thousand at your right hand, but it shall not come near you. Only a spectator shall you be [yourself inaccessible in the secret place of the Most High] as you witness the reward of the wicked Because you have made the Lord your refuge, and the Most High your dwelling place, there shall no evil befall you, nor any plague or calamity come near your tent." (Psalm 91:7-10 AMP)

The problems in the world will not be able to overcome you when you are in God's presence. Cling to God expectantly whenever you face adversity. "The Lord also will be a refuge and a high tower for the oppressed, a refuge and a stronghold in times of trouble (high cost, destitution, and desperation)." (Psalm 9:9 AMP)

We have included this verse of Scripture because of the words "high cost, destitution, and desperation" in the amplification. Difficult times are coming upon the world. All of the signs are here. We do not know when severe adversity is coming, but we do know that it is coming.

Regardless of how difficult the economy may be or how desperate people may be, you *will* be protected if you know God intimately, trust Him completely and remain in the safety of His presence. "...in the shadow of Your wings will I take refuge and be confident until calamities and destructive storms are passed." (Psalm 57:1 AMP)

Once again when this verse speaks of being in God's shadow, it refers to being in God's presence. You will be filled with unwavering faith in God when you are in His presence. If you are in His presence when storms come at you, you will be absolutely certain that He will protect you until the storms have passed. "...whoever leans on, trusts in, and puts his confidence in the Lord is safe and set on high." (Proverbs 29:25 AMP)

The word "whoever" includes *you*. When you are in God's presence, you will trust Him completely. He will lift you safely above whatever problems you face.

The last two chapters have been filled with glorious truth from the holy Scriptures pertaining to the presence of God. If you understand the vital importance of being in the presence of God, you will *not* allow anyone or anything to come ahead of your fervent desire to do exactly what your Father has instructed you to do to continually come into and remain in His presence.

Chapter 29

Pride Will Block You from Intimacy with God

There is a definite relationship between pride, humility and intimacy with God. Most proud people have an exaggerated opinion of their own importance. Proud people often think that they are too good to reach out to help people whom they consider to be inferior to them.

Your Father wants you to be more than willing to do everything you can to help others. If you believe that you are superior to anyone and you refuse to reach out, you are doing exactly what Satan wants you to do. "...if any person thinks himself to be somebody [too important to condescend to shoulder another's load] when he is nobody [of superiority except in his own estimation], he deceives and deludes and cheats himself." (Galatians 6:3 AMP)

You deceive yourself if you are so puffed up with pride that you do not reach out to help others who are less fortunate than you are. "...do not be haughty (snobbish, high-minded, exclusive), but readily adjust yourself to [people, things] and give yourselves to humble tasks. Never overestimate yourself or be wise in your own conceits." (Romans 12:16 AMP)

Your Father does not want you to be filled with pride. He does not want you to look down on other people. He wants you to consistently put Him first, other people second and yourself last. Your Father wants every aspect of your life to revolve around your deep and sincere desire to serve Him and to serve others. You should be like Jesus Who said, "I receive not glory from men [I crave no human honor, I look for no mortal fame]" (John 5:41 AMP)

Your perspective on life should not be based on what other people think of you. Your perspective should be based on what God thinks of you. Do not crave recognition from other people because you want them to be impressed with you. You were created to serve God and to help others.

All sin is rooted in pride and selfishness. Can you think of one sin that is not rooted in selfishness which comes from pride? Pride was the original sin that caused Satan and his demons to fall from heaven (see Isaiah 14:12-15 and I Timothy 3:6).

Pride blocks you from knowing God. Pride elevates self. You must elevate God above yourself if you truly desire an intimate relationship with Him.

Christians who draw close to God are humble, reverent and child-like in their trust in God. Christians who have a difficult time coming close to God often are proud, self-centered and intellectual.

As you consistently draw closer to God, you will realize how inadequate you are. Your Father wants you to turn to Him at all times with simple childlike trust because you know how much you need His help.

Pride gives Satan and his demons a foothold in your life. If you sincerely desire a close relationship with God, your mind and your heart should be filled with truths from God's Word about the vital importance of being truly humble. "Woe to those who are wise in their own eyes and clever in their own sight." (Isaiah 5:21 NIV)

If you are puffed up with pride, you are headed for trouble. God emphasizes through repetition. His Word repeatedly tells you that you ultimately will bring severe problems upon yourself if you are proud. "Pride goeth before destruction, and an haughty spirit before a fall." (Proverbs 16:18 KJV)

Proud people *will* pay a price for their pride – the only question is when, not if. "The Lord detests all the proud of heart. Be sure of this: They will not go unpunished." (Proverbs 16:5 NIV)

God despises pride. Proud people sit on the throne of their lives where God is meant to sit. They are their own little gods.

Proud people who seem to have everything are headed for big problems. They ultimately will be punished for their pride. They will not receive the blessings that God reserves for His children who are humble. "…He gives His undeserved favor to the low [in rank], the humble, and the afflicted." (Proverbs 3:34 AMP)

You cannot earn and you do not deserve God's grace. God gives His grace to His humble children. "He guides the humble in what is right and teaches them his way." (Psalm 25:9 NIV)

Humble Christians turn to God for the guidance that He promises to give them. Humble Christians are teachable. They want to learn from God. They consistently study and meditate on His Book of Instructions, the Bible. Jesus said, "Blessed (happy, to be envied, and spiritually prosperous—with life-joy and satisfaction in God's favor and salvation, regardless of their outward conditions) are the poor in spirit (the humble, who rate themselves insignificant), for theirs is the kingdom of heaven!" (Matthew 5:3 AMP)

You will be blessed by God if you do not have a puffed up view of yourself. Humble Christians are much happier and more satisfied than people who are proud.

You should be determined to humble yourself before God and other people. "…in the true spirit of humility (lowliness of mind) let each regard the others as better than and superior to himself [thinking more highly of one another than you do of yourselves]. Let each of you esteem and look upon and be concerned for not [merely] his own interests, but also each for the interests of others. Let this same attitude and purpose and [humble] mind be in you which was in Christ Jesus: [Let Him be your example in humility:]" (Philippians 2:3-5 AMP)

You should never look down on others. You should look at other people as being *better* than you are and *superior* to you. Turn away from selfish goals. Devote your life to serving God and other people. Jesus Christ is your example in every area of life. You should be like Jesus was throughout His earthly ministry.

At one time Satan was an archangel named Lucifer who was very close to God. Lucifer was so proud that he wanted to be ascend above God (see Isaiah 14:12-17). God cast Satan and legions of angels out of heaven because of their pride (see Ezekiel 28:17). Satan and his demons want you to fall into the same trap that they did. They will try to influence you to "...develop a beclouded and stupid state of mind] as the result of pride [be blinded by conceit, and] fall into the condemnation that the devil [once] did." (I Timothy 3:6 AMP)

Your thinking will be cloudy if you are proud. People who are proud are stupid. They are headed for the same fall that Satan and his demons took. You must not make this mistake. "...God sets Himself against the proud and haughty, but gives grace [continually] to the lowly (those who are humble enough to receive it)." (James 4:6 AMP)

Do you want your Father to set Himself against you? Of course you don't. Do you want God to give you grace continually? You decide throughout every day of your life whether you will cause God to oppose you or to give you the grace that He reserves for His humble children. "...Clothe (apron) yourselves, all of you, with humility [as the garb of a servant, so that its covering cannot possibly be stripped from you, with freedom from pride and arrogance] toward one another. For God sets Himself against the proud (the insolent, the overbearing, the disdainful, the presumptuous, the boastful)—[and He opposes, frustrates, and defeats them], but gives grace (favor, blessing) to the humble." (I Peter 5:5 AMP)

You should cover yourself with humility just as you cover your body with clothing. You should have such a servant's heart that nothing can cause you to swell with selfish pride.

Can you understand that Almighty God will set Himself against you if you are proud? Proud people oppose God. God hates pride so much that He causes proud people to be frustrated. Pride ultimately causes people to be defeated.

Your Father does not want to treat you this way. He will pour out favor, grace and blessings on you if you are humble. "Therefore humble yourselves [demote, lower yourselves in your own estimation] under the mighty hand of God, that in due time He may exalt you" (I Peter 5:6 AMP)

Jesus Christ will lift you up if you truly are humble. If Jesus is your Savior, you are a beloved child of God (see John 1:12-13, Romans 8:9, II Corinthians 6:18, Galatians 3:26, Ephesians 2:18-19 and I John 3:1). You are unique and special.

If you surrender your whole being to God, you will become more than you ever imagined you could be. "...though the Lord is high, yet has He respect to the lowly [bringing them into fellowship with Him]; but the proud and haughty He knows and recognizes [only] at a distance." (Psalm 138:6 AMP)

Consistent humility will bring you into God's presence. You will fellowship with God. If you are proud, you will keep God at a distance.

God is omniscient. He knows exactly how much pride is in every one of each of the billions of people on earth. Ask God to reveal to you whenever you do something that is caused by pride. If the Holy Spirit shows you that you have done something that is proud, admit your pride. Repent of this pride. Ask your Father to forgive you. Jesus said, "Whoever exalts himself [with haughtiness and empty pride] shall be humbled (brought low), and whoever humbles himself [whoever has a modest opinion of himself and behaves accordingly] shall be raised to honor." (Matthew 23:12 AMP)

You decide throughout every day of your life whether you will be lifted up in the spiritual realm or brought down. Refuse to allow Satan and his demons to influence your thinking to cause you to be proud. Humble yourself continually before God and before others. Your Father will lift you up.

This chapter is filled with truth from the Bible regarding pride and humility. If you have a tendency to be proud, you should meditate on these verses of Scripture. Strengthen yourself in the spiritual realm by consistently focusing on your Father's repeated instructions to humble yourself before Him and before others. Enjoy your Father. He loves you.

Your Father yearns for a close and intimate relationship with you. Do not allow pride to block you from receiving this wonderful blessing. Consistently humble yourself before God and before others.

Chapter 30

Revere God and Hold Him in Constant Awe

In this chapter we will look into the Bible to learn the relationship between fearing God and enjoying a close and intimate relationship with Him. When you fear God, you revere Him and adore Him. You are in constant awe of His majesty. "Blessed is every one that feareth the LORD; that walketh in his ways." (Psalm 128:1 KJV)

You will be blessed if you truly fear God and if you consistently do your best to learn and to faithfully obey the instructions in His Word. "...Blessed is the man who fears the LORD, who finds great delight in his commands. His children will be mighty in the land; the generation of the upright will be blessed. Wealth and riches are in his house, and his righteousness endures forever." (Psalm 112:1-3 NIV)

Do you delight in the Word of God? Do you love God's Word so much that you cannot get enough of it? Does your heart sing with joy as you consistently learn great spiritual truths from the supernatural Word of God (see Jeremiah 15:16)?

This verse of Scripture says that you and your family will be blessed if you truly fear God and if you delight in His Word. "...Fear God [revere and worship Him, knowing that He is] and keep His commandments, for this is the whole of man [the full, original purpose of his creation, the object of God's providence, the root of character, the foundation of all happiness, the adjustment to all inharmonious circumstances and conditions under the sun] and the whole [duty] for every man." (Ecclesiastes 12:13 AMP)

Once again you are instructed to fear God and to faithfully obey the instructions in His Word. Do you believe that doing what God created you to do is vitally important? God created you to fear Him. Every aspect of your life should revolve your constant reverence for God and your awe of Him.

The degree of intimacy that you have with God is directly related to your fear of God. Your character is directly related to your fear of God. Your happiness is directly related to your fear of God. Your ability to adjust to adversity is directly related to your fear of God. "Let all the earth fear the Lord [revere and worship Him]; let all the inhabitants of the world stand in awe of Him." (Psalm 33:8 AMP)

God wants *every* person in the world to stand in awe of Him. When God creates people, He puts fear for Him in their hearts. God said, "...I will put My [reverential] fear in their hearts, so that they will not depart from Me." (Jeremiah 32:40 AMP)

Every person is born with the fear of God in his or her heart. However, God gives each person He creates freedom of choice. You decide throughout your life whether you will truly fear God. If you do, you will stay close to Him at all times. "The secret [of the sweet, satisfying companionship] of the Lord have they who fear (revere and worship) Him..." (Psalm 25:14 AMP)

This verse of Scripture explains *the secret* of enjoying an intimate relationship with God. You can only be close to God to the degree that you consistently fear Him, revere Him and worship Him. "Oh, how great is Your goodness, which You have laid up for those who fear, revere, and worship You, goodness which You have wrought for those who trust and take refuge in You before the sons of men!" (Psalm 31:19 AMP)

God always emphasizes through repetition. Once again you are told that you will be blessed if you fear God. If you truly revere God you will trust Him completely. You will be so close to Him that you will be absolutely certain that He will protect you at all times. "The Lord is near to all who call upon Him, to all who call upon Him sincerely and in truth. He will fulfill the desires of those who rever ently and worshipfully fear Him; He also will hear their cry and will save them." (Psalm 145:18-19 AMP)

If you truly fear God, He will be close to you and you will be close to Him. If you fear God, He will answer your prayers. He will fulfill the desires of your heart.

The following words that Solomon spoke to his son apply to you today. "My son, if you will receive my words and treasure up my commandments within you, making your ear attentive to skillful and godly Wisdom and inclining and directing your heart and mind to understanding [applying all your powers to the quest for it]; yes, if you cry out for insight and raise your voice for understanding, if you seek [Wisdom] as for silver and search for skillful and godly Wisdom as for hidden treasures, then you will understand the reverent and worshipful fear of the Lord and find the knowledge of [our omniscient] God." (Proverbs 2:1-5 AMP)

This passage of Scripture explains that you should look at God's Word as a magnificent spiritual treasure. You should faithfully obey your Father's instructions to consistently study and meditate on His Word so that your mind and your heart will be filled with Scripture.

If your mind and your heart are filled with God's Word, you will be tuned in to God's wisdom. You will yearn to consistently receive more wisdom from God. If you consistently seek God's wisdom, you will understand what the reverent fear of God is. You will consistently draw closer to God.

If you fear God and hold Him in reverent awe at all times, the Holy Spirit Who lives in the heart of every person who has asked Jesus Christ to be his or her Savior will give you supernatural guidance. "...the Spirit of the Lord shall rest upon Him—the Spirit of wisdom and understanding, the Spirit of counsel and might, the Spirit of knowledge and of the reverential and obedient fear of the Lord" (Isaiah 11:2 AMP)

The Holy Spirit has infinite wisdom and understanding. He always knows what to do. He will advise you and guide you if you stay close to God because of your reverent awe for Him. "In the reverent and worshipful fear of the Lord there is strong confidence, and His children shall always have a place of refuge." (Proverbs 14:26 AMP)

If you consistently revere, worship and fear God, you will have deep, strong and unwavering faith in Him. You will be able to enter into the supernatural place of refuge that your Father has provided for all of His children.

Immature Christians do not hold God in constant and reverent awe. Mature Christians focus on the majesty and grandeur of God. They fear Him, revere Him and trust Him completely. "The fear of the LORD tendeth to life: and he that hath it shall abide satisfied; he shall not be visited with evil." (Proverbs 19:23 KJV)

If you truly fear God, you will be fulfilled, satisfied and content deep down within yourself. The word "evil" in this verse of Scripture refers to Satan and his demons. Satan and his demons have no difficulty influencing unbelievers and some Christians. Satan and his demons will not be able to exert their evil influence on you if you truly fear God. "…by the reverent, worshipful fear of the Lord men depart from and avoid evil." (Proverbs 16:6 AMP)

We often remind you that God emphasizes through repetition. Both of these Scripture references from the Book of Proverbs say that reverently fearing God will block Satan and his demons from being able to influence you. "…the Lord's eye is upon those who fear Him [who revere and worship Him with awe], who wait for Him and hope in His mercy and loving-kindness, to deliver them from death and keep them alive in famine." (Psalm 33:18-19 AMP)

God focuses continually on His children who truly fear Him. If you fear God and trust Him completely, He promises to deliver you from death and to keep you alive when you face severe problems during your life on earth. "'Do not forget the covenant I have made with you, and do not worship other gods. Rather, worship the LORD your God; it is he who will deliver you from the hand of all your enemies.' They would not listen, however, but persisted in their former practices." (II Kings 17:38-40 NIV)

This passage of Scripture refers to the Israelites in the wilderness who placed other gods ahead of the Lord God. The Israelites did not listen even though God had promised to deliver them from their enemies if they feared Him.

This same principle applies to you today. *You decide* whether God will deliver you from the enemies you face. If you truly fear God, you can be certain that He will bring you safely through whatever Satan, his demons and any human enemies will attempt to do to you.

You must not make the mistake that the Israelites made. You should fear God at all times. Every aspect of your life should revolve around your certainty of His magnificent indwelling presence. "...The Angel of the Lord encamps around those who fear Him [who revere and worship Him with awe] and each of them He delivers." (Psalm 34:7 AMP)

Please note the capitalization of the word "Angel" in this verse of Scripture. Scholars have different opinions, but we believe that this word refers to Jesus Christ. The word "encamps" in this context is similar to a place where soldiers set up camp.

Jesus will establish a spiritual place of protection around you if you truly fear God, revere Him and worship Him. He will deliver you from whatever adversity you face. If you truly fear God, you will have an intimate relationship with Him. You will trust Him completely regardless of the seeming severity of any adversity you face. "You who [reverently] fear the Lord, trust in and lean on the Lord! He is their Help and their Shield." (Psalm 115:11 AMP)

God will help you if you fear Him. He will protect you. Fearing God should be a way of life to you. "...continue in the reverent and worshipful fear of the Lord all the day long." (Proverbs 23:17 AMP)

This chapter is filled with great scriptural truths about fearing God. You should be *so* devoted to God that you revere Him and hold Him in constant awe at all times. If you truly fear God, He will be in absolute first place in your life and you will continually draw closer to Him.

Chapter 31

Learn How to Hear God's Voice

Your Father has given you the ability to hear Him speaking to you. You should listen expectantly for His voice. Jesus said, "He who has ears to hear, let him be listening and let him consider and perceive and comprehend by hearing." (Matthew 11:15 AMP)

Jesus refers here to Christians who are able to hear God. If Jesus Christ is your Savior, you have been given the ability to hear God speak to you. Jesus said, "...Be careful what you are hearing. The measure [of thought and study] you give [to the truth you hear] will be the measure [of virtue and knowledge] that comes back to you — and more [besides] will be given to you who hear." (Mark 4:24 AMP)

You should be very careful what you allow to come into your ears. Many people are unduly influenced by what they hear on radio, on television and in movies. I (Jack) go to an extreme level in this area. When Jesus tells me to be careful what I am hearing, I am determined to obey His instruction. The only things I watch on television are weather forecasts, sports and Christian programming. I mute all commercials. I do not listen to the radio.

As we mentioned previously, we have more than one hundred Gaither worship videos and DVDs. I have watched many of them five or more times. We have a carefully selected group of movies on VHS and DVDs that I watch in addition to the Gaither videos.

Some Christians have no concept of what they are allowing to come into their ears from television, movies and radio. They continually allow their ears to be filled with material that is directly opposed to what the Bible teaches.

The best thing for your ears to hear is your voice repeatedly speaking the Word of God with deep, bold and unwavering faith. If you obey your Father's instructions to meditate day and night on His Word, your ears will hear your voice consistently speaking God's Word as you speak the Scripture verses you are meditating on.

God's Word is a spiritual seed (see Luke 8:11). You plant spiritual seeds in the spiritual soil of your heart when you meditate on the Word of God. As your ears hear your mouth continually speaking God's Word, you enable yourself to receive more revelation from God. The amount of thought and focus that you put into studying and meditating on the Bible will determine how much revelation you will receive in return.

You can learn a great deal if you are a good listener. This principle applies in the natural realm and in the spiritual realm. You learn in the natural realm by listening to those who have knowledge you want to attain. You learn in the spiritual realm by listening to God speak to you. "…Let every man be quick to hear [a ready listener], slow to speak, slow to take offense and to get angry." (James 1:19 AMP)

You should listen continually for God's voice. Instead of talking a lot, you should be slow to speak, particularly if you are tempted to be angry.

God is omniscient and omnipresent. He knows every language and dialect. He is able to speak to all of His children throughout the world. No matter what country you live in or what language you speak, God speaks your language.

You are righteous before God if Jesus Christ is your Savior. This righteousness enables you to hear God's voice when you could not hear Him before you were saved. Jesus said, "Whoever is of God listens to God. [Those who belong to God hear the words of God.] This is the reason that you do not listen [to those words, to Me]: because you do not belong to God and are not of God or in harmony with Him." (John 8:47 AMP)

Unbelievers cannot hear God. They cannot tune in to His voice. They are not on His wavelength. All Christians have been given the ability to hear God's voice. Unfortunately, some Christians do not hear what God is saying because their preoccupation with the things of the world blocks them from hearing what God is saying to them.

You cannot hear God's voice unless you have an intimate relationship with Him. Faithfully obey the scriptural instructions you are reading in this book that explain how to draw close to God. *Know* that God speaks to you throughout every day of your life because His Word says that He does.

The same God Who spoke clearly to many people in the Bible still speaks clearly to people today. You must be humble and teachable. Christians who are not humble and teachable have a hard heart. A hard heart will block you from hearing God speaking to you. "…Today, if you will hear His voice, do not harden your hearts, as [happened] in the rebellion [of Israel] and their provocation and embitterment [of Me] in the day of testing in the wilderness" (Hebrews 3:7-8 AMP)

You must not be like the Israelites who blocked themselves from hearing God because of the hardness of their hearts when they were in the wilderness. Instead of having a hard heart, you should listen with eager expectation for the voice of God.

You should be like sheep that respond eagerly to the voice of their shepherd. Jesus said, "The man who enters by the gate is the shepherd of his sheep. The watchman opens the gate for him, and the sheep listen to his voice. He calls his own sheep by name and leads them out. When he has brought out all his own, he goes on ahead of them, and his sheep follow him because they know his voice. But they will never follow a stranger; in fact, they will run away from him because they do not recognize a stranger's voice." (John 10:2-5 NIV)

Sheep know their shepherd's voice. They react to his voice. This same principle applies to you in the spiritual realm. Jesus Christ is your Shepherd. You need to listen to His voice and then do what He is telling you to do. Jesus said, "The sheep that are My own hear and are listening to My voice; and I know them, and they follow Me." (John 10:27 AMP)

When Jesus speaks of His sheep, He is speaking of people who have received Him as their Savior. If Jesus is your Savior, you should listen for His voice just as intently as sheep listen for the voice of their shepherd.

Christians who know Jesus intimately are able to hear Him speaking to them. They know that Jesus is with them at all times and that He will guide them continually if they will listen to Him.

The Word of God is the key to hearing the voice of Jesus Christ. If you faithfully obey your Father's instructions to renew your mind each day by studying His Word and to meditate day and night on His Word, you will consistently program yourself to hear His voice much more clearly. Jesus said, "...Everyone who is of the Truth [who is a friend of the Truth, who belongs to the Truth] hears and listens to My voice." (John 18:37 AMP)

When Jesus speaks of the Truth, He speaks of the Word of God which is the Truth (see John 17:17). There is a definite relationship between how consistently you study and meditate on the Word of God and how clearly you hear Jesus speaking to you. Christians who love the Word of God cannot get enough of God's Word. They immerse themselves in the Word of God throughout every day and night of their lives.

Hearing God's voice can be compared to tuning in to a radio station. There are many voices from television channels and radio stations in the atmosphere around you at all times, but you can only hear these voices if you are tuned to a specific frequency. God's voice is similar. God speaks to you continually, but you must learn how to get on His spiritual wavelength. You tune into God's voice through what could be referred to as the spiritual radio station WORD.

The more time you spend in God's Word, the better you will be able to hear Him speaking to you. God is like a twenty-four hour radio station. He is omniscient and omnipresent. He knows everything. He can be in an infinite number of places at the same time. God is able to speak directly to every one of His children throughout the world.

If you sincerely desire to hear God speaking to you, you must *know* that you can tune into His voice by studying and meditating on His Word. If you consistently study and meditate on the Word of God, you will take more and more of God's written Word from the printed pages of the Bible and place this Scripture into your mind and your heart. You then will be able to hear God's voice much more clearly.

You should approach your daily Bible study and Scripture meditation with an attitude of expectancy. Expect God to give you magnificent spiritual revelation as you obey His instructions to consistently study and meditate on His Word. Your ears will be quickened to His voice.

You should increase your daily Scripture meditation when you face adversity and you need to hear God's voice. Joshua 1:8 and Psalm 1:2 instruct you to meditate day and night on God's Word. We believe that this instruction means that you should meditate *during* each day and night when everything is going well and *throughout* the day and night when you face adversity.

You should fine tune your Scripture meditation so that the Scripture you are meditating on applies directly to whatever challenges you face in your life. Our book, *What Does God Say?*, categorizes 1,221 verses of Scripture into 94 topics. You can program your Scripture meditation by choosing selected topics from this book.

You also can program your Scripture meditation from our ten sets of fifty-two Scripture Meditation Cards. Each set of Scripture cards deals with specific biblical topics such as overcoming worry and fear, receiving healing from sickness, and living in God's peace. Also each of our books contain an abundance of Scripture that has been carefully arranged by topic. (See the order form at the back of this book or on our website.)

The amount of God's Word that lives in your mind and your heart is cumulative. If you have spent many months and years studying and meditating on God's Word, you have a *large amount* of the Word of God on deposit in your mind and your heart. If you have programmed yourself continually with God's Word, you will have Scripture on several different topics living inside of you. You will be able to reach down inside of yourself to pull up appropriate Scripture to fit many needs.

This ability enables you to hear God speaking specifically to you in whatever area you need His help. If you need physical healing, you need to know what God's Word says about healing. The more you meditate on healing Scripture, the better you will be able to hear your Father speaking to you.

If you face financial challenges, you need to know what God's Word says about God's provision and your Father meeting all of your needs. As you study and meditate on these specific passages of Scripture, you will be able to hear God speaking to you in this area.

In this chapter we have given you general instructions on hearing the voice of God. In the next chapter we will give you more specific instructions that will tell you exactly what to do to hear your Father's voice.

Chapter 32

Listen to God's Voice
When You Face Adversity

The Bible is filled with accounts of God speaking to His people. If God spoke to them, you can be certain that He will speak to you. God does not play favorites. "…God shows no partiality [undue favor or unfairness; with Him one man is not different from another]." (Romans 2:11 AMP)

Expect your Father to speak to you continually just as He spoke to many people in the Bible. You should be like Samuel who said, "…Speak, Lord, for Your servant is listening." (I Samuel 3:10 AMP)

Stay close to God. Set aside precious quiet time to be alone with Him each day. God does not speak to you only during this quiet time. You tune in to Him during your quiet time so that you can hear Him speaking to you at any time of the day or night. If you have paid the price of tuning into God's voice through His Word, you will hear His voice on many occasions telling you exactly what you need to know at that particular time.

You can only hear God's voice to the degree that you are quiet, calm and confident deep down within yourself. You cannot afford to allow agitation, worry, fear or other negative emotions to block you from hearing God's voice.

In previous chapters you read many scriptural truths pertaining to quiet time with God. Turn away from the world each day to turn toward God. Turn off the television set. Turn away from external influences. Turn within yourself where God lives.

I (Jack) have found that I often hear God's voice clearly when I am exercising or soon after I finish. I have walked vigorously almost every day for the past thirty-eight years. I always carry a memo pad and pen in my pocket. I often stop walking to write down what I hear God saying to me.

Muscular fatigue is an effective tranquilizer. Exercise draws blood away from your brain, quiets your mind and relaxes your body. Exercise is conducive to hearing the voice of God more clearly.

As you hear God speaking to you more frequently, you will be able to identify His voice. People who are very close to you do not need to identify themselves when they call you on the phone. You will instantly recognize the voice of these people. This same principle applies to hearing the voice of God.

We recommend that you have paper and pen with you at all times. Carry a memo pad in your pocket or purse. Keep a pad on the nightstand next to your bed. Expect to hear God speaking to you at unusual times.

You may hear God speaking to you when you are taking a shower, dressing or doing something else that is routine. You should be prepared to hear what God is saying at any time of the day or night and to instantly write down what He says.

You will find that, if you do not instantly write down what God says, you will not be able to retain this thought for very long. We have learned over the years the vital importance of writing down what God says immediately. Do not experience the frustration of having God speak to you and losing this precious thought because you forgot what God said.

You do not need to learn how to hear the voices of Satan and his demons. They speak to people all over the world continually. No special education or training is required to hear Satan speaking.

Satan is the god of this world (see II Corinthians 4:4 and I John 5:19). He speaks very clearly to everyone. Satan and his demons continually try to put thoughts into the minds of believers and unbelievers.

Satan and his demons speak loudly and emphatically. God speaks quietly. Satan and his demons who have no spiritual power (see Luke 10:19) will try to force their voices into your consciousness. God Who is omnipotent and filled with power speaks softly. You must be quiet and still within yourself to hear God's voice which is referred to in the Bible as "...a still, small voice." (I Kings 19:12 AMP)

God with all of His power speaks quietly and softly to you. He is looking for His children who are eager to hear Him and are quiet, calm and trusting within themselves.

Christians who have spent little or no quiet time with God frequently will accelerate this time when they face severe adversity. Adversity often causes people to change their focus from the things of the world to the things of God. "He delivers the afflicted in their affliction and opens their ears [to His voice] in adversity." (Job 36:15 AMP)

Your Father promises to deliver you when you face trials and tribulations (see Isaiah 43:2-3). You often will be able to hear God much more clearly when you have turned away from preoccupation with the things of the world to draw closer to Him because you face adversity.

God will speak to you in different ways at different times. Sometimes you will awaken during the night to hear God speaking to you. You often will hear God's voice very clearly immediately after awakening in the morning. "[One may hear God's voice] in a dream, in a vision of the night, when deep sleep falls on men while slumbering upon the bed" (Job 33:15 AMP)

We believe that very difficult times are coming upon the world. If there ever was a time when you need to hear the voice of God, we live in that time. Your Father knows exactly what will happen in the future. He will tell you how to prepare for the future if you will learn how to tune in to His voice and listen to and obey His instructions.

Everyone will need to learn how to hear God's voice when the world faces widespread adversity. Prepare yourself now by learning and obeying the scriptural instructions in this book that will help you to draw closer to God so that you will be able to hear His voice.

God very seldom will speak to you audibly. As you learn how to hear God's voice in your spirit, you will know when He is speaking to you. You will have an inner certainty that you are hearing from God.

Each time that you hear from God, you will be more likely to hear His voice in the future. Christians who have had a close and intimate relationship with God for many years hear God speak to them continually. Hearing His voice is a vitally important part of their daily lives.

You will experience a breakthrough in your relationship with God if you obey the scriptural instructions in this book. As you begin to hear God speaking to you, you will want to hear from Him even more. Listen continually for God's voice throughout each day and night of your life.

Your Father has given you specific instructions telling you how He wants you to live. He instructs you to pray without ceasing (see I Thessalonians 5:17). His Word tells you to praise Him throughout the day and night (see Psalm 113:3). The Bible instructs you to meditate day and night on the holy Scriptures (see Joshua 1:8 and Psalm 1:2-3).

God provided a Book of Instructions to tell you exactly how He wants you to live. Faithfully obey these instructions. You will be able to hear God's voice much more clearly if you consistently obey the specific instructions He has given you in the Bible.

You must know how to receive guidance from God during the difficult times that will be coming upon the world (see II Timothy 3:1). The next chapter is filled with specific instructions from the Word of God that will tell you how to receive the invaluable guidance that your Father very much wants to give you.

Chapter 33

God Will Guide You Continually

Your loving Father will guide you throughout every day of your life. You can only receive His guidance if you have such a close and intimate relationship with Him that you trust Him completely. "Lean on, trust in, and be confident in the Lord with all your heart and mind and do not rely on your own insight or understanding. In all your ways know, recognize, and acknowledge Him, and He will direct and make straight and plain your paths." (Proverbs 3:5-6 AMP)

God will show you exactly what He wants you to do. Your Father has promised to guide you. He will do His part. You must do your part.

Your part is to consistently turn away from the limitations of human understanding to trust God completely. Your part is to acknowledge Him in every area of your life. *Are you* doing these things? If you are, you will receive invaluable direction from God.

God has put the Holy Spirit in your heart to be your guide. If you consistently study and meditate on God's Word, you will receive guidance from the Holy Spirit. "…I will put my Spirit within you and cause you to walk in My statutes, and you shall heed My ordinances and do them." (Ezekiel 36:27 AMP)

The Holy Spirit will guide you in direct proportion to the amount of God's Word that fills your mind and your heart. He will show you how to live your life in continual obedience to God's instructions in the Bible.

If you have faithfully obeyed your Father's instructions to renew your mind each day and to fill your heart with His Word by meditating on it day and night, you will have programmed yourself with the essentials that are required for the Holy Spirit to guide you. "...to us God has unveiled and revealed them by and through His Spirit, for the [Holy] Spirit searches diligently, exploring and examining everything, even sounding the profound and bottomless things of God [the divine counsels and things hidden and beyond man's scrutiny]. For what person perceives (knows and understands) what passes through a man's thoughts except the man's own spirit within him? Just so no one discerns (comes to know and comprehend) the thoughts of God except the Spirit of God." (I Corinthians 2:10-11 AMP)

The Holy Spirit will remove the spiritual veil that blocks many people from understanding the ways of God. He will reveal great spiritual truths to you if you consistently turn to God with a humble and teachable heart.

You should pray as the apostle Paul prayed for the Ephesians when he said, "[For I always pray to] the God of our Lord Jesus Christ, the Father of glory, that He may grant you a spirit of wisdom and revelation [of insight into mysteries and secrets] in the [deep and intimate] knowledge of Him, by having the eyes of your heart flooded with light, so that you can know and understand the hope to which He has called you, and how rich is His glorious inheritance in the saints (His set-apart ones)." (Ephesians 1:17-18 AMP)

This passage of Scripture explains the relationship between an intimate relationship with God and your heart being filled with light. Light often refers to God in the Bible and darkness often refers to Satan. God's Word is light.

You cannot know God intimately if your heart is not filled with the light of His Word as a result of consistent Scripture meditation. If your heart is filled with the light of God's Word, "...the Lord will grant you full insight and understanding in everything." (II Timothy 2:7 AMP)

God is very explicit here. The words "full" and "everything" are declarative and emphatic. If your heart is filled with the light of God's

Word, you will have programmed yourself to receive supernatural understanding from God. You can trust God to guide you at all times.

Only those who consistently seek God with every fiber of their being can comprehend what are mysteries to others. God reveals His heart to His children who yearn for an intimate relationship with Him because they love Him wholeheartedly.

The following words that Jesus spoke to His disciples apply to your life today. Jesus said, "…when He, the Spirit of Truth (the Truth-giving Spirit) comes, He will guide you into all the Truth (the whole, full Truth). For He will not speak His own message [on His own authority]; but He will tell whatever He hears [from the Father; He will give the message that has been given to Him], and He will announce and declare to you the things that are to come [that will happen in the future]." (John 16:13 AMP)

The Holy Spirit continually works in conformity to the truth of God's Word. He will guide you by utilizing the Word of God that you have stored in your heart.

The Holy Spirit knows exactly what the future holds. You can trust Him to guide you today and throughout the future. "…thine ears shall hear a word behind thee, saying, This is the way, walk ye in it, when ye turn to the right hand, and when ye turn to the left." (Isaiah 30:21 KJV)

In the Old Testament the voice of God often is spoken of as being outside of you. This verse of Scripture says that you will hear His voice "behind" you. If Jesus Christ is your Savior, the Holy Spirit lives within you. You will hear His voice from within yourself.

He will tell you when to turn to the left and when to turn to the right. He will guide you throughout every day of your life to the degree that you are tuned in to hear His voice. "…those who are led by the Spirit of God are sons of God." (Romans 8:14 NIV)

If Jesus Christ is your Savior, you are a child of God. As a child of God, you have been given the opportunity to be led by the Holy Spirit throughout every day of your life. "…walk and live [habitually] in the [Holy] Spirit [responsive to and controlled and guided by the Spirit]…" (Galatians 5:16 AMP)

The word "habitually" in this verse of Scripture is very important. Guidance from the Holy Spirit should be a way of life to you. Ideally, you should yield control of every area of your life to the Holy Spirit so that He can guide you continually. "...the LORD shall guide thee continually..." (Isaiah 58:11 KJV)

There is no time that divine guidance is not available to you. You should be like the psalmist who said, "...I am continually with You; You do hold my right hand. You will guide me with Your counsel..." (Psalm 73:23-24 AMP)

The word "continually" is used in both of these verses of Scripture. Your Father wants you to know that He is with you at all times and that He will guide you throughout every day of your life if you will turn away from your God-given right to control your life and willingly yield control to Him.

Little children are very secure when they are holding tightly to the hand of their father or mother. Your heavenly Father will hold your hand in the spiritual realm just as He held the hand of the psalmist. God said, "I will lead the blind by ways they have not known, along unfamiliar paths I will guide them; I will turn the darkness into light before them and make the rough places smooth. These are the things I will do; I will not forsake them." (Isaiah 42:16 NIV)

God can see many things that you cannot see. When you are on the wrong path, He will lead you to the right path if you listen to Him. He will smooth out the rough edges along the way. He wants to guide you throughout every day of your life. "...this God is our God for ever and ever: he will be our guide even unto death" (Psalm 48:14 KJV)

God promises to guide you continually right up to the day that you leave this earth to be with Him in heaven. God will guide you in everything you do. He also will guide and anoint every word that comes out of your mouth. Jesus said, "...do not worry about what to say or how to say it. At that time you will be given what to say, for it will not be you speaking, but the Spirit of your Father speaking through you." (Matthew 10:19-20 NIV)

Do *not* worry about what you will say when you face a difficult predicament and the words that you speak are very important. You can have absolute faith that the Holy Spirit will speak through you giving you the words that you need exactly when you need them.

This chapter contains many truths from the Bible about the supernatural guidance that God has made available to *you*. We hope that you are encouraged by these great spiritual truths.

God has a definite plan for every day of your life. We now are ready to look into God's Word for revelation about the guidance that God promises to help you to do exactly what He has called you to do with your life.

Chapter 34

Seek God's Will for Your Life

In the last three chapters you have learned great truths from the Bible about hearing God's voice and receiving guidance from God. We now are ready to learn why all Christians who have an intimate relationship with God are able to consistently yield control of their lives to God. Living this way does not come naturally to us. "...everyone looks out for his own interests, not those of Jesus Christ." (Philippians 2:21 NIV)

All of us were born as descendants of Adam with a selfish desire to control our lives. When Jesus Christ becomes your Savior, you are given the opportunity to live for Him. As you grow and mature in Jesus and draw closer to Him, you will have a continually increasing desire to turn away from selfish goals to live your life the way that Jesus wants you to live. "...He died for all, so that all those who live might live no longer to and for themselves, but to and for Him Who died and was raised again for their sake." (II Corinthians 5:15 AMP)

Jesus died and rose from the dead so that your life would not be focused upon selfish desires. As you grow and mature spiritually, you will become highly motivated to live a life that is totally dedicated to Him.

Jesus paid an enormous price so that you can devote your life to doing what He has called you to do. Your life does not belong to you – it belongs to Jesus. "For none of us lives to himself alone and none of us dies to himself alone. If we live, we live to the Lord; and if we die, we die to the Lord. So, whether we live or die, we belong to the Lord." (Romans 14:7-8 NIV)

Both of these passages of Scripture emphasize that your life should be completely devoted to doing what God wants you to do. "…You are not your own, you were bought with a price [purchased with a preciousness and paid for, made His own]. So then, honor God and bring glory to Him in your body." (I Corinthians 6:19-20 AMP)

God continues to emphasize through repetition, telling you for a third time that your life does not belong to you. Your life belongs to Jesus because of the immense price that He paid when He shed His precious blood to pay for all of your sins.

As you continue to grow and mature in God, you will have a deep desire to seek, find and carry out His will for your life. "…The God of our forefathers has destined and appointed you to come progressively to know His will [to perceive, to recognize more strongly and clearly, and to become better and more intimately acquainted with His will]…" (Acts 22:14 AMP)

The word "progressively" in this verse of Scripture is very important. When you do something progressively, you do whatever you are doing in stages. God often will reveal His plan for your life a little at a time. He may show you His general plan originally, but He usually will unfold the details of His specific plan for your life incrementally as you continue to draw closer to Him.

You have seen that God makes His home in the heart of every person who has received Jesus Christ as his or her Savior. "…it is God Who is all the while effectually at work in you [energizing and creating in you the power and desire], both to will and to work for His good pleasure and satisfaction and delight." (Philippians 2:13 AMP)

God will give you the energy, power and desire to seek, find and carry out His assignment for your life. You will give your Father great pleasure and satisfaction if you fervently pursue His plan for your life.

You have learned that, as you consistently draw closer to God, you will be able to hear His voice more clearly. As your relationship with God continues to become more intimate, you will hear many additional details from your Father explaining exactly what He desires you to do with your life.

Jesus is your example in every area of your life. Jesus was totally committed throughout His earthly ministry to do exactly what His Father had sent Him to earth to do. He said, "...I do not seek or consult My own will [I have no desire to do what is pleasing to Myself, My own aim, My own purpose] but only the will and pleasure of the Father Who sent Me." (John 5:30 AMP)

All of the people in the Bible who did great things for God had one thing in common – they each had an intimate personal relationship with God. If Jesus Christ is your Savior, you have been brought into a spiritual position where you will be given the opportunity to seek, find and carry out God's will for your life. "...we are God's [own] handiwork (His workmanship), recreated in Christ Jesus, [born anew] that we may do those good works which God predestined (planned beforehand) for us [taking paths which He prepared ahead of time], that we should walk in them [living the good life which He prearranged and made ready for us to live]." (Ephesians 2:10 AMP)

This verse of Scripture explains the relationship between receiving Jesus as your Savior and doing what God has called you to do with your life. Please note that God had a definite plan for your life *before* He created you. The psalmist David knew that God had a specific plan for every day of his life before he was born. David said, "Your eyes saw my unformed substance, and in Your book all the days [of my life] were written before ever they took shape, when as yet there was none of them." (Psalm 139:16 AMP)

God is omniscient. He knows every minute detail pertaining to every one of the lives of the billions of people He has created. God, speaking to the prophet Jeremiah, said, "Before I formed you in the womb I knew [and] approved of you [as My chosen instrument], and before you were born I separated and set you apart, consecrating you; [and] I appointed you as a prophet to the nations." (Jeremiah 1:5 AMP)

God had a plan for Jeremiah's life before He formed him in his mother's womb. God does not play favorites (see Acts 10:34). If God had a special plan for the lives of David and Jeremiah before He creatcd thcm, you can bc ccrtain that Hc had a dcfinite plan for *your* life before He created you.

God creates each person with the special gifts and talents that will be required to carry out His plan for this person's life. You should be determined to use the talents that God has given you to serve Him and to help others. "We have different gifts, according to the grace given us. If a man's gift is prophesying, let him use it in proportion to his faith. If it is serving, let him serve; if it is teaching, let him teach; if it is encouraging, let him encourage; if it is contributing to the needs of others, let him give generously; if it is leadership, let him govern diligently; if it is showing mercy, let him do it cheerfully." (Romans 12:6-8 NIV)

As you continually draw closer to God, He will reveal more and more of His specific plan for your life. "Do not, therefore, fling away your fearless confidence, for it carries a great and glorious compensation of reward. For you have need of steadfast patience and endurance, so that you may perform and fully accomplish the will of God, and thus receive and carry away [and enjoy to the full] what is promised." (Hebrews 10:35-36 AMP)

Your Father wants you to have absolute confidence that He does have a definite plan for your life. He will reward you bountifully if you are patient and persevering in seeking to fully accomplish the assignment He has given to you.

You can be certain that your faith in God will be challenged on many occasions if you persistently pursue His will. Keep moving forward. Refuse to give up.

If you have a deep and sincere desire to seek, find and carry out God's plan for your life, you must have a continual consciousness of His indwelling presence. Every aspect of your life should be focused on your absolute certainty that God Himself lives in your heart and that He will speak to you and guide you continually.

This chapter is filled with scriptural truth about surrendering control of your life so that God can guide you to carry out His plan for your life. For more biblical help on finding God's will for your life see our Scripture Meditation Cards titled *Find God's Will for Your Life* and the accompanying CDs. Also see Judy's link on our website, www.lamplight.net. In the next chapter we will look into God's Word for additional instructions on surrendering control of your life to God so that His plan for your life will be fully and completely accomplished.

Chapter 35

Surrender Your Desire to Control Your Life

There is no question that your Father does not want you to control your life. No matter how much human ability you may have, He wants you to yield to Him. "...the way of a man is not in himself; it is not in man [even in a strong man or in a man at his best] to direct his [own] steps." (Jeremiah 10:23 AMP)

Sometimes having a great deal of God-given ability can be a detriment, not an asset. No matter how gifted and talented you may be, your Father does not want you to control your life.

God gave you the Holy Spirit to live in your heart to guide you continually. He wants you to trust completely in the Holy Spirit instead of trusting in your human abilities, no matter how great they may seem. "...Having begun [your new life spiritually] with the [Holy] Spirit, are you now reaching perfection [by dependence] on the flesh?" (Galatians 3:3 AMP)

You receive the Holy Spirit when you receive Jesus Christ as your Savior (see Romans 8:9). Ideally, you should yield to Him immediately after becoming a Christian. However, many Christians revert back to their previous habits and attempt to control their own lives. You must understand that great things in the spiritual realm are accomplished through you, not by you. "...'Not by might nor by power, but by my Spirit,' says the LORD Almighty." (Zechariah 4:6 NIV)

You will not attempt to control your life if you can even begin to comprehend the supernatural power and ability of the Holy Spirit

Who lives in the heart of every Christian. Why would you ever attempt to control your life with your limited human abilities when the Holy Spirit Who lives in your heart is ready, willing and able to control your life? You must willingly yield control to Him. "The steps of a [good] man are directed and established by the Lord when He delights in his way [and He busies Himself with his every step]." (Psalm 37:23 AMP)

God wants to direct you every step of the way. He is delighted when you gladly yield control of your life to Him. You should be like the apostle Paul who knew that his life no longer belonged to him. Paul referred to himself as "…I Paul, the prisoner of Jesus Christ…" (Ephesians 3:1 KJV)

People who are in prison are not there willingly. They are sent to prison for their crimes. Paul *willingly* became a prisoner of Jesus Christ. He gladly relinquished control of his life to Jesus. Paul said, "…I die daily [I face death every day and die to self]." (I Corinthians 15:31 AMP)

Paul emphasized that he died to his selfish desires throughout every day of his life. As you grow and mature as a Christian and continually draw closer to God, you will die more and more to self-centeredness and the pursuit of selfish goals. You will be like Paul who said, "I have been crucified with Christ [in Him I have shared His crucifixion]; it is no longer I who live, but Christ (the Messiah) lives in me; and the life I now live in the body I live by faith in (by adherence to and reliance on and complete trust in) the Son of God, Who loved me and gave Himself up for me." (Galatians 2:20 AMP)

You should crucify all selfish desires. Your life should be completely devoted to giving up control of your life to trust completely in the indwelling Jesus Christ to live His life in you and through you. Jesus said, "…If any person wills to come after Me, let him deny himself [disown himself, forget, lose sight of himself and his own interests, refuse and give up himself] and take up his cross daily and follow Me [cleave steadfastly to Me, conform wholly to My example in living and, if need be, in dying also]." (Luke 9:23 AMP)

Do you deeply desire to do what Jesus wants you to do with your life? Will you deny all selfish desires to yield to the victorious Jesus

Christ Who lives in your heart? Will you give up these selfish desires just as Jesus gave up His life for you?

Jesus wants you to get out of the driver's seat. Trust Him completely to guide you every step of the way. Surrender control to Jesus every day. Continually draw closer to Him.

God has given you the Holy Spirit to guide you continually. "…live and move not in the ways of the flesh but in the ways of the Spirit [our lives governed not by the standards and according to the dictates of the flesh, but controlled by the Holy Spirit]. For those who are according to the flesh and are controlled by its unholy desires set their minds on and pursue those things which gratify the flesh, but those who are according to the Spirit and are controlled by the desires of the Spirit set their minds on and seek those things which gratify the [Holy] Spirit." (Romans 8:4-5 AMP)

If you have yielded control to the Holy Spirit, you are doing what God has called you to do. '…you are living the life of the Spirit, if the [Holy] Spirit of God [really] dwells within you [directs and controls you]…." (Romans 8:9 AMP)

God always emphasizes through repetition. Your Father repeatedly tells you that He does not want you to be in control of your life. Once again God emphasizes that He wants the Holy Spirit Who lives in your heart to direct and control your life.

You cannot successfully accomplish God's assignment for your life if you depend solely on your human abilities because you will be limited to the natural realm. The Holy Spirit will guide you and control you if you let go and trust Him completely.

We have previously studied Ephesians 5:18 where you are instructed to constantly be filled with the Holy Spirit. You can only be filled with the Holy Spirit to the degree that you are empty of self.

Rev. Dwight Moody was an American evangelist who founded the Moody Bible Institute in Chicago. He also conducted many revival campaigns in England. Rev. Moody once said, "A great many think because they are filled once they are going to be filled for all time afterward. My friends, we are leaky vessels and have to keep right under the fountain all the time in order to keep full."

Yielding your life to the Holy Spirit is not a one-time occurrence. Throughout every hour of every day of your life you should draw closer to God and surrender more and more to the Holy Spirit. "...the fruit of the Spirit is love, joy, peace, patience, kindness, goodness, faithfulness, gentleness and self-control...." (Galatians 5:22-23 NIV)

If the Holy Spirit controls your life, He will produce spiritual fruit in you and through you. Love, joy, peace, patience, kindness, goodness, faithfulness, gentleness and self-control are fruit of the Holy Spirit. Yield to the Holy Spirit. Trust Him completely to produce supernatural fruit in you and through you.

If you continually draw closer to God, you will experience more and more of the Holy Spirit in your life. You will be calmer and quieter. You will be more loving. You will be filled with joy. You will be patient. All of the fruit of the Spirit will be produced in your life.

Some people think that they will give up their freedom if they surrender control of their lives to the Holy Spirit. Just the opposite is true. Freedom in the spiritual realm comes from gladly allowing the Holy Spirit to control your life.

Many of the problems that most people experience come from living a self-centered life. The Holy Spirit will set you free from these problems to the degree that you yield control of your life to Him. "Now the Lord is the Spirit, and where the Spirit of the Lord is, there is freedom." (II Corinthians 3:17 NIV)

You cannot begin to understand the totality of God's will for your life with your limited human comprehension. You must understand that God's plan assignment for you will include many tasks that are far beyond the limitations of your human abilities.

The Holy Spirit can and will do everything in you and through you that must be done to successfully complete God's plan for your life. The Holy Spirit can see into the future. He knows many things that you cannot possibly know.

There is a definite relationship between developing a closer and deeper relationship with God and the lessening of your desire to control your life. The more intimately you know God, the less desire you will have to control your life. If you do not die to selfish desires, you will not be able to consistently enjoy a deeper relationship with God.

Unfortunately, many Christians live and die without ever having taken advantage of the glorious privilege they have been given to draw closer to God. The last two chapters have clearly shown you what God can and will do in you and through you *if* you will seek His will wholeheartedly and *if* you will gladly yield control of your life to Him, trusting completely in Him and His indwelling presence throughout every day of your life.

Conclusion

This book contains hundreds of scriptural truths pertaining to a close and intimate relationship with God. There is a definite connection between the intimacy of your relationship with God and the length and quality of your life. "...love the Lord your God, obey His voice, and cling to Him. For He is your life and the length of your days..." (Deuteronomy 30:20 AMP)

Do you want to live a long, full and meaningful life? God controls the length and quality of your life. If you love Him, obey Him and cling to Him, you will live a long and fulfilling life.

You must understand the absolute necessity of staying close to God. We have repeatedly stated our belief that very difficult times are coming upon the world. Almost all Christian leaders agree that our generation is living in the final days before Jesus Christ returns for His church.

We have previously studied II Timothy 3:1. This verse of Scripture prophesies that very difficult times will come upon the world during the last days before the return of Jesus Christ.

If there ever has been a time to draw closer to God, we live in that time. You cannot afford to waste precious time and energy on trivial worldly pursuits. You must have a deep and strong desire to constantly draw closer to God.

You will not be able to cope with the severe adversity that is coming upon the world if you only have a casual relationship with God or no relationship at all. People who do not have an intimate relationship with God will find that the upcoming years will be extremely difficult.

When little children face a difficult problem, they come as close to their parents as they possibly can. You should do the same with your heavenly Father. Prepare now for the difficult times that are coming by learning and faithfully obeying the scriptural instructions in this book that tell you exactly what to do to develop a close and intimate relationship with God.

Nothing that the world offers can remotely compare with the magnificent blessings that you will experience if you have a deep and intimate personal relationship with God. Every person in heaven will enjoy this wonderful relationship throughout eternity. Jesus has provided you with the opportunity to experience a wonderful preview now of the relationship you will experience in heaven.

The detailed Study Guide at the end of this book will enable you to measure yourself very clearly as to how close you are to God. The following list of questions is not intended to be that specific. However, you can carefully review the following eighteen questions for an *immediate* indication of how well you are doing in drawing closer to God.

QUESTION   YOUR ANSWER

1. Do you *yearn* for a close and intimate relationship
    with God? .... _____

2. Are you absolutely *certain* that God desires a close and
    intimate relationship with you regardless of your faults
    and shortcomings? .... _____

3. Do you *know* that God is your loving Father and that
    you are His beloved child? .... _____

4. Are you certain that God lives in your heart and that He
    is *with you* throughout every minute of every hour of
    every day? .... _____

5. Do you consistently do your best to put Jesus Christ in
    first place, other people in second place and yourself in
    last place? .... _____

6. Are you setting aside specific quiet time *each* day to
    draw closer to God? .... _____

7. Do you *delight* in the Word of God? Are you *meditating* day and night on God's Word? .... _____

8. Are you doing your best to consistently learn and *obey* the specific instructions your Father has given to you in His supernatural Book of Instructions? .... _____

9. Do you trust God *completely* with simple childlike trust because you have such a close and intimate relationship with Him? .... _____

10. Are you doing your very best at all times to focus on *God* instead of focusing on whatever problems you face? .... _____

11. Are you praying *continually*, especially for other people? .... _____

12. Do you *thank* God and *praise* Him continually? .... _____

13. Do you consistently *sing* praises to God? .... _____

14. Are you doing your very best to learn how to come into God's presence and *remain* there? .... _____

15. Do you *fear* God and *humble* yourself before Him and other people? .... _____

16. Are you continually *hearing* God's voice guiding you? .... _____

17. Do you continually seek to find and carry out *God's will* for your life? .... _____

18. Are you consistently *yielding control* of your life to the Holy Spirit? .... _____

Your answers to these questions will show you now whether or not you have a close relationship with God. If you have answered all or most of these questions affirmatively, keep doing what you are doing. If not, please go back to the beginning of this book and carefully meditate on Scripture pertaining to the areas where you could not answer affirmatively. Program yourself to do exactly what your Father has instructed you to do to continually draw closer to Him.

We pray that this book has been a blessing to you. We love you and we would be so blessed to hear from you. Our hearts sing with joy when we hear that what we have written and what we have presented from the Bible has made a difference in someone's life.

Jack and Judy

Appendix

This book is filled with instructions and promises from God. However, if you have not received Jesus Christ as your Savior, you *cannot understand* the scriptural facts that are contained in this book. "...the mind of the flesh [with its carnal thoughts and purposes] is hostile to God, for it does not submit itself to God's Law; indeed it cannot." (Romans 8:7 AMP)

Please highlight or underline the word "cannot" in this verse of Scripture. If Jesus Christ is not your Savior, you cannot understand and obey God's instructions.

People who have not received Jesus Christ as their Savior are not open to the specific instructions God has given us in the Bible. "...the natural, nonspiritual man does not accept or welcome or admit into his heart the gifts and teachings and revelations of the Spirit of God, for they are folly (meaningless nonsense) to him; and he is incapable of knowing them [of progressively recognizing, understanding, and becoming better acquainted with them] because they are spiritually discerned and estimated and appreciated." (I Corinthians 2:14 AMP)

The words "does not accept or welcome or admit into his heart the gifts and teachings and revelations of the Spirit of God" in this verse of Scripture are very important. Some people are strongly opposed to the Bible and what it teaches. They look at facts from the Bible as "meaningless nonsense." These people are incapable of learning great spiritual truths from God until and unless they receive Jesus Christ as their Savior.

At the close of this Appendix we will explain exactly what you should do to receive Jesus Christ as your Savior. If and when you make this decision, the glorious supernatural truths of the Bible will open up to you. Jesus said, "…To you it has been given to know the secrets and mysteries of the kingdom of heaven, but to them it has not been given." (Matthew 13:11 AMP)

Jesus was speaking to *you* when He said that you can "know the secrets and mysteries of the kingdom of heaven." You must not miss out on the glorious privilege that is available to every believer to know and understand the ways of God.

A spiritual veil blocks all unbelievers from understanding the things of God. "…even if our Gospel (the glad tidings) also be hidden (obscured and covered up with a veil that hinders the knowledge of God), it is hidden [only] to those who are perishing and obscured [only] to those who are spiritually dying and veiled [only] to those who are lost." (II Corinthians 4:3 AMP)

When and if you receive Jesus Christ as your Savior, this spiritual veil will be pulled aside. "…whenever a person turns [in repentance] to the Lord, the veil is stripped off and taken away." (II Corinthians 3:16 AMP)

If you obey the scriptural instructions at the end of this Appendix, Jesus Christ will become your Savior. Everything in your life will become fresh and new. "…if any person is [ingrafted] in Christ (the Messiah) he is a new creation (a new creature altogether); the old [previous moral and spiritual condition] has passed away. Behold, the fresh and new has come!" (II Corinthians 5:17 AMP)

Instead of being opposed to the teachings of the holy Bible, you will be completely open to these teachings. You will have a hunger and thirst to continually learn more truth from the supernatural living Word of God. "…I endorse and delight in the Law of God in my inmost self [with my new nature]." (Romans 7:22 AMP)

Every person who has not received Jesus Christ as his or her Savior is a sinner who is doomed to live throughout eternity in the horror of hell. God has made it possible for *you* to escape this terrible eternal penalty. "…God so loved the world, that he gave his only begotten Son, that whosoever believeth in him should not perish, but have everlasting life." (John 3:16 KJV)

God knew that everyone who lived on earth after Adam and Eve would be a sinner because of the sins of Adam and Eve (see Romans 3:10-12). He sent His only Son to take upon Himself the sins of the world as He died a horrible death by crucifixion. If you believe that Jesus Christ paid the full price for *your* sins and if you trust Him completely for your eternal salvation, you will live eternally in the glory of heaven.

There is only *one* way for you to live eternally in heaven after you die – that is to receive eternal salvation through Jesus Christ. "Jesus saith unto him, I am the way, the truth, and the life: no man cometh unto the Father, but by me." (John 14:6 KJV)

If you trust in anyone or anything except Jesus Christ for your eternal salvation, you will not live eternally in heaven. If you are reading these facts about living eternally in heaven because of the price that Jesus Christ has paid for you, you must understand that the same God Who created you actually is drawing you to come to Jesus Christ for eternal salvation. Jesus said, "No one is able to come to Me unless the Father Who sent Me attracts and draws him and gives him the desire to come to Me…" (John 6:44 AMP)

Are you interested in these facts about where you will live throughout eternity? If you are, you can be certain that the same awesome God Who created you is drawing you to Jesus Christ at this very minute.

Heaven is a glorious place. Everyone in heaven is completely healthy and totally happy. "…God shall wipe away all tears from their eyes; and there shall be no more death, neither sorrow, nor crying, neither shall there be any more pain: for the former things are passed away. (Revelation 21:4 KJV)

All of the problems of earth will disappear when you go to heaven. No one in heaven dies. No one in heaven is sad. No one in heaven cries. No one in heaven suffers from pain.

When you die you will live eternally in one place or another. If you do not receive Jesus Christ as your Savior, you will live eternally in hell. People in hell will experience continual torment throughout eternity. "...the smoke of their torment ascendeth up for ever and ever: and they have no rest day nor night..." (Revelation 14:11 KJV)

Everyone in heaven is filled with joy. Everyone in hell is miserable. Jesus described what hell would be like when He said, "...there will be weeping and wailing and grinding of teeth. (Matthew 13:42 AMP)

Throughout eternity the inhabitants of hell will weep and wail. They will grind their teeth in anguish. Can you imagine living this way for the endless trillions of years of eternity? This is exactly what will happen to *you* if Jesus Christ is not your Savior.

How do you receive eternal salvation through Jesus Christ? "...if you acknowledge and confess with your lips that Jesus is Lord and in your heart believe (adhere to, trust in, and rely on the truth) that God raised Him from the dead, you will be saved. For with the heart a person believes (adheres to, trusts in, and relies on Christ) and so is justified (declared righteous, acceptable to God), and with the mouth he confesses (declares openly and speaks out freely his faith) and confirms [his] salvation." (Romans 10:9-10 AMP)

You must *believe in your heart* (not just think in your mind) that Jesus paid the full price for all of your sins when He was crucified. You must believe that God raised Jesus from the dead. You must open your mouth and *speak this truth* that you believe in your heart. If you believe in your heart that Jesus Christ died and rose again from the dead and that the price for your sins has been paid for and you tell others that you believe this great spiritual truth, you *have* been saved and you *will* live eternally in heaven.

If Jesus Christ was not your Savior when you began to read this book, we pray that He is your Savior now. Your life will change immensely. You will never be the same again. Every aspect of your life will be gloriously new.

Please let us know if you have become a child of God by receiving eternal salvation through Jesus Christ. We would like to pray for you and welcome you as our new brother or sister in Christ Jesus. We love you and bless you in the name of our Lord Jesus Christ.

We would be so pleased to hear from you. If you are already a believer, we would be pleased to hear from you as well. We invite you to visit our website at www.lamplight.net. Please let us know if this book or one or more of our other publications has made a difference in our life. Please give us your comments so that we can share these comments in our newsletters and on our website to encourage other people.

Study Guide

What Did You Learn from This Book?

The questions in this Study Guide are carefully arranged to show you how much you have learned about a close and intimate relationship with God. This Study Guide is not intended to be an academic test. The sole purpose of the following questions is to help you increase your *practical knowledge* pertaining to a more intimate relationship with God.

Page Reference

1. Many biblical promises are conditional. God has promised to come close to you, but you must do your part. What does God require from you before He will come close to you? (James 4:8) 25

2. Can you be absolutely certain that God really does desire an intimate relationship with you? (Hebrews 6:18 and Joshua 23:14) 26

3. How did Jesus Christ emphasize the importance that He places on having a close relationship with you? (Revelation 3:20) 26-27

4. What are you instructed to do to establish a higher life that consists of a close relationship with God? (Matthew 10:39, I Corinthians 6:17 and Jeremiah 9:24) 27-28

5. Why does the same God Who created heaven, earth, the moon and the stars desire an intimate relationship with you with your faults and shortcomings? Do your sins prohibit you from enjoying a close relationship with God? (Psalm 8:3-4 and Isaiah 59:2) 29

6. At one time Adam and Eve enjoyed an intimate relationship with God. What did they do that separated them

A Few Words About Lamplight Ministries

Lamplight Ministries, Inc. originally began in 1983 as Lamplight Publications. After ten years as a publishing firm with a goal of selling Christian books Lamplight Ministries was founded in 1993. Jack and Judy Hartman founded Lamplight Ministries with a mission of continuing to sell their publications and also to *give* large numbers of these publications free of charge to needy people all over the world.

Lamplight Ministries was created to allow people who have been blessed by our publications to share in financing the translation, printing and distribution of our books into other languages and also to distribute our publications free of charge to jails and prisons. Over the years many partners of Lamplight Ministries have shared Jack and Judy's vision. As the years have gone by Lamplight Ministries' giving has increased with each passing year. Thousands of people in jails and prisons and in Third World countries have received our publications free of charge.

Our books and Scripture Meditation Cards have been translated into eleven foreign languages – Armenian, Danish, Greek, Hebrew, German, Korean, Norwegian, Portuguese, Russian, Spanish and the Tamil dialect in India. The translations in these languages are not available from Lamplight Ministries in the United States. These translations can only be obtained in the countries where they have been printed.

The pastors of many churches in Third World countries have written to say that they consistently preach sermons in their churches based on the scriptural contents of our publications. We believe that people in several churches in many different countries consistently hear sermons that are based on the scriptural contents of our publications. Praise the Lord!

Jack Hartman was the sole author of twelve Christian books. After co-authoring one book with Judy, Jack and Judy co-authored ten sets of Scripture Meditation Cards. Judy's contributions to *God's Wisdom Is Available To You*, *Exchange Your Worries for God's Perfect Peace*, *Unshakable Faith in Almighty God*, *Receive Healing from the Lord*, *What Does God Say?*, *Victory over Adversity* and *God's Joy Regardless of Circumstances* were so significant that she is the co-author of these books. Jack and Judy currently are working on other books that they believe the Lord is leading them to write as co-authors.

We invite you to request our newsletters to stay in touch with us, to learn of our latest publications and to read comments from people all over the world. Please write, fax, call or email us. You are very special to us. We love you and thank God for you. Our heart is to take the gospel to the world and for our books to be available in every known language. Hallelujah!

Lamplight Ministries, Inc.,

PO Box 1307 - Dunedin, Florida, 34697. USA

Phone: 1-800-540-1597 • Fax: 1-727-784-2980

website: lamplight.net • email: lamplight@lamplight.net

We offer you a substantial quantity discount

From the beginning of our ministry we have been led of the Lord to offer the same quantity discount to individuals that we offer to Christian bookstores. Each individual has a sphere of influence with a specific group of people. We believe that you know many people who need to learn the scriptural contents of our publications.

The Word of God encourages us to give freely to others. We encourage you to give selected copies of these publications to people you know who need help in the specific areas that are covered by our publications. See our order form for specific information on the quantity discounts that we make available to you so that you can share our books, Scripture Meditation Cards and CDs with others.

A request to our readers

If this book has helped you, we would like to receive your comments so that we can share them with others. Your comments can *encourage other people* to study our publications to learn from the scriptural contents of these publications.

When we receive a letter containing comments on any of our books, cassette tapes or Scripture Meditation Cards, we prayerfully take out excerpts from these letters. These selected excerpts are included in our newsletters and occasionally in our advertising and promotional materials.

If any of our publications have been a blessing to you, please share your comments with us so that we can share them with others. Tell us in your own words what a specific publication has meant to you and why you would recommend it to others. Please give as much specific information as possible. We prefer three or four paragraphs so that we can condense this into one paragraph.

Thank you for taking a few minutes of your time to encourage other people to learn from the scripture references in our publications.

ORDER FORM FOR BOOKS

Book Title	Quantity	Total
What Does God Say? ($18)	_____ x $18 =	_____
A Close and Intimate Relationship with God ($14)	_____ x $14 =	_____
God's Joy Regardless of Circumstances ($14)	_____ x $14 =	_____
Victory Over Adversity ($14)	_____ x $14 =	_____
Receive Healing from the Lord ($14)	_____ x $14 =	_____
Unshakable Faith in Almighty God ($14)	_____ x $14 =	_____
Exchange Your Worries for God's Perfect Peace ($14)	_____ x $14 =	_____
God's Wisdom is Available to You ($14)	_____ x $14 =	_____
Trust God For Your Finances ($10)	_____ x $10 =	_____
What Will Heaven Be Like? ($10)	_____ x $10 =	_____
Quiet Confidence in the Lord ($10)	_____ x $10 =	_____
Never, Never Give Up ($10)	_____ x $10 =	_____
Increased Energy and Vitality ($10)	_____ x $10 =	_____
God's Will for Our Lives ($10)	_____ x $10 =	_____
How to Study the Bible ($7)	_____ x $7 =	_____
Nuggets of Faith ($7)	_____ x $7 =	_____
100 Years From Today ($7)	_____ x $7 =	_____

Price of books _____

Minus 40% discount for 5-9 books _____

Minus 50% discount for 10 or more books _____

Net price of order _____

Add 15% **before discount** for shipping and handling _____

Florida residents only, add 7% sales tax _____

Tax deductible contribution to Lamplight Ministries, Inc. _____

Enclosed check or money order (do not send cash) _____
(Foreign orders must be submitted in U.S. dollars.)

Please make check payable to **Lamplight Ministries, Inc**. and mail to:
PO Box 1307, Dunedin, FL 34697

MC____ Visa____ AmEx____ Disc.____ Card # _____

Exp Date _____ Signature _____

Name _____

Address _____

City _____

State or Province _____ Zip or Postal Code _____

ORDER FORM FOR BOOKS

Book Title	Quantity	Total
What Does God Say? ($18)	_____ x $18 =	_____
A Close and Intimate Relationship with God ($14)	_____ x $14 =	_____
God's Joy Regardless of Circumstances ($14)	_____ x $14 =	_____
Victory Over Adversity ($14)	_____ x $14 =	_____
Receive Healing from the Lord ($14)	_____ x $14 =	_____
Unshakable Faith in Almighty God ($14)	_____ x $14 =	_____
Exchange Your Worries for God's Perfect Peace ($14)	_____ x $14 =	_____
God's Wisdom is Available to You ($14)	_____ x $14 =	_____
Trust God For Your Finances ($10)	_____ x $10 =	_____
What Will Heaven Be Like? ($10)	_____ x $10 =	_____
Quiet Confidence in the Lord ($10)	_____ x $10 =	_____
Never, Never Give Up ($10)	_____ x $10 =	_____
Increased Energy and Vitality ($10)	_____ x $10 =	_____
God's Will for Our Lives ($10)	_____ x $10 =	_____
How to Study the Bible ($7)	_____ x $7 =	_____
Nuggets of Faith ($7)	_____ x $7 =	_____
100 Years From Today ($7)	_____ x $7 =	_____

Price of books   _____

Minus 40% discount for 5-9 books   _____

Minus 50% discount for 10 or more books _____

Net price of order   _____

Add 15% **before discount** for shipping and handling _____

Florida residents only, add 7% sales tax _____

Tax deductible contribution to Lamplight Ministries, Inc. _____

Enclosed check or money order (do not send cash) _____
(Foreign orders must be submitted in U.S. dollars.)

Please make check payable to **Lamplight Ministries, Inc**. and mail to:
PO Box 1307, Dunedin, FL 34697

MC____ Visa____ AmEx____ Disc.____ Card # _____

Exp Date _____ Signature _____

Name _____

Address _____

City _____

State or Province _____ Zip or Postal Code _____

ORDER FORM FOR SCRIPTURE MEDITATION CARDS AND CDs

SCRIPTURE MEDITATION CARDS	QUANTITY	PRICE
Find God's Will for Your Life ($5)	_____	_____
Financial Instructions from God ($5)	_____	_____
Freedom from Worry and Fear ($5)	_____	_____
A Closer Relationship with the Lord ($5)	_____	_____
Our Father's Wonderful Love ($5)	_____	_____
Receive Healing from the Lord ($5)	_____	_____
Receive God's Blessing in Adversity ($5)	_____	_____
Enjoy God's Wonderful Peace ($5)	_____	_____
God is Always with You ($5)	_____	_____
Continually Increasing Faith in God ($5)	_____	_____

CDs	QUANTITY	PRICE
Find God's Will for Your Life ($10)	_____	_____
Financial Instructions from God ($10)	_____	_____
Freedom from Worry and Fear ($10)	_____	_____
A Closer Relationship with the Lord ($10)	_____	_____
Our Father's Wonderful Love ($10)	_____	_____
Receive Healing from the Lord ($10)	_____	_____
Receive God's Blessing in Adversity ($10)	_____	_____
Enjoy God's Wonderful Peace ($10)	_____	_____
God is Always with You ($10)	_____	_____
Continually Increasing Faith in God ($10)	_____	_____

TOTAL PRICE _____

Minus 40% discount for 5-9 Scripture Cards and CDs _____
Minus 50% discount for 10 or more Scripture Cards and CDs _____
Net price of order _____
Add 15% **before discount** for shipping and handling _____
Florida residents only, add 7% sales tax _____
Tax deductible contribution to Lamplight Ministries, Inc. _____
Enclosed check or money order (do not send cash) _____
(Foreign orders must be submitted in U.S. dollars.)

Please make check payable to **Lamplight Ministries, Inc**. and mail to:
PO Box 1307, Dunedin, FL 34697

MC____ Visa____ AmEx____ Disc.____ Card # _____

Exp Date _____ Signature _____

Name _____

Address _____

City _____

State or Province _____ Zip or Postal Code _____

ORDER FORM FOR SCRIPTURE MEDITATION CARDS AND CDs

SCRIPTURE MEDITATION CARDS	QUANTITY	PRICE
Find God's Will for Your Life ($5)	_____	_____
Financial Instructions from God ($5)	_____	_____
Freedom from Worry and Fear ($5)	_____	_____
A Closer Relationship with the Lord ($5)	_____	_____
Our Father's Wonderful Love ($5)	_____	_____
Receive Healing from the Lord ($5)	_____	_____
Receive God's Blessing in Adversity ($5)	_____	_____
Enjoy God's Wonderful Peace ($5)	_____	_____
God is Always with You ($5)	_____	_____
Continually Increasing Faith in God ($5)	_____	_____

CDs	QUANTITY	PRICE
Find God's Will for Your Life ($10)	_____	_____
Financial Instructions from God ($10)	_____	_____
Freedom from Worry and Fear ($10)	_____	_____
A Closer Relationship with the Lord ($10)	_____	_____
Our Father's Wonderful Love ($10)	_____	_____
Receive Healing from the Lord ($10)	_____	_____
Receive God's Blessing in Adversity ($10)	_____	_____
Enjoy God's Wonderful Peace ($10)	_____	_____
God is Always with You ($10)	_____	_____
Continually Increasing Faith in God ($10)	_____	_____

TOTAL PRICE _____

Minus 40% discount for 5-9 Scripture Cards and CDs _____

Minus 50% discount for 10 or more Scripture Cards and CDs _____

Net price of order _____

Add 15% **before discount** for shipping and handling _____

Florida residents only, add 7% sales tax _____

Tax deductible contribution to Lamplight Ministries, Inc. _____

Enclosed check or money order (do not send cash) _____

(Foreign orders must be submitted in U.S. dollars.)

Please make check payable to **Lamplight Ministries, Inc.** and mail to:
PO Box 1307, Dunedin, FL 34697

MC____ Visa____ AmEx____ Disc.____ Card # _____

Exp Date _____ Signature _____

Name _____

Address _____

City _____

State or Province _____ Zip or Postal Code _____